FINANCIAL MANAGERS

PRACTICAL CAREER GUIDES

Series Editor: Kezia Endsley

FINANCIAL MANAGERS

A Practical Career Guide

MARCIA SANTORE

ROWMAN & LITTLEFIELD
Lanham • Boulder • New York • London

Published by Rowman & Littlefield
An imprint of The Rowman & Littlefield Publishing Group, Inc.
4501 Forbes Boulevard, Suite 200, Lanham, Maryland 20706
www.rowman.com

6 Tinworth Street, London, SE11 5AL, United Kingdom

British Library Cataloguing in Publication Information Available

Library of Congress Cataloging-in-Publication Data

Names: Santore, Marcia, 1960– author.
Title: Financial managers : a practical career guide / Marcia Santore.
Description: Lanham : Rowman & Littlefield, [2021] | Series: Practical
  career guides | Includes bibliographical references. | Summary:
  "Financial Managers: A Practical Career Guide includes interviews with
  professionals in a field that has proven to be a stable, lucrative, and
  growing profession"—Provided by publisher.
Identifiers: LCCN 2021001596 (print) | LCCN 2021001597 (ebook) | ISBN
  9781538152058 (paperback) | ISBN 9781538152065 (epub)
Subjects: LCSH: Corporations—Finance. | Financial executives. | Chief
  financial officers.
Classification: LCC HG4014 .S36 2021 (print) | LCC HG4014 (ebook) | DDC
  658.15023—dc23
LC record available at https://lccn.loc.gov/2021001596
LC ebook record available at https://lccn.loc.gov/2021001597

♾™ The paper used in this publication meets the minimum requirements of American National Standard for Information Sciences—Permanence of Paper for Printed Library Materials, ANSI/NISO Z39.48-1992.

Contents

Introduction

So You Want a Career as a Financial Manager

Welcome to a career as a financial manager!

- Do you like to work with numbers?
- Do you like to work with people?
- Are you good at details, charts, graphs, projections, and reports?
- Are you willing to work hard and put in the hours?
- Do you want to be a vital part of your institution's success?
- Do you want a well-paying career with opportunities for advancement?

If you answered "Yes!" to these questions, you might want to be a financial manager.

Careers for Financial Managers

So many different jobs are covered by the title "financial manager." The opportunities are wide open! You could work for a bank, a manufacturing company, a financial services company, the health industry, the insurance industry, or a nonprofit organization like a university, hospital, or major charitable organization.

You could be the one who tracks and manages cash flow. Or the one who helps the company make good decisions about how to use or extend credit. Or the one who evaluates which risks are worth taking and which to avoid. Or the one who is in charge of all the financial action going on in your organization.

As a financial manager, you'll help ensure your company's financial stability. *PeopleImages/E+/Getty Images*

The Job Market for Financial Managers

The field of financial management is stable and growing. It includes many roles to play—some you might not have thought of before, some you might never even have heard of! Depending on where you plan to live and work, all kinds of financial management jobs rely on people who can understand numbers, calculate risk, make projections, track the flow of finances, and communicate all of that information to their team and their clients.

What Does This Book Cover?

In this book, you'll get a general overview of what different kinds of financial managers do and what to expect at different stages of your career. Each chapter represents a step in your journey.

CHAPTER 1: WHY CHOOSE A CAREER AS A FINANCIAL MANAGER?

In the first chapter, you'll learn about a few of the types of financial manager jobs that are out there. In this book, we'll focus on a few of those careers, including the following:

- Bank managers
- Cash managers
- Chief financial officers
- Compliance managers
- Controllers
- Credit managers
- Fund managers
- International finance managers
- Insurance managers
- Risk managers

You'll get a good idea of what each type of financial manager career is like, required skills, working conditions, work schedule, and what you could expect to earn in each of those roles. You'll also learn a little bit about jobs that are similar to financial managers or use some of the same skills.

CHAPTER 2: FORMING A CAREER PLAN

The second chapter is all about you and how you can plan a career as a financial manager. What do you need to know about yourself? If you're just starting out, how can you make your time in high school and college work for you? If you're already working and looking to change careers or move up to a financial manager role, what do you need to know? Where can you find more information?

Having a plan helps keep you on the right track toward your goals. Chapter 2 will show you how to think about who you are, what you're good at, and what matters to you. You'll also learn about how to figure out whether the career you're considering matches you and your personality.

CHAPTER 3: PURSUING THE EDUCATION PATH

In the third chapter, you'll learn about the education path to follow to become a financial manager. This chapter covers such things as finding the right college or university, choosing your degree plan, and important things to know about financial aid.

You'll learn about undergraduate degrees that help you get your foot in the door and graduate degrees and professional certification that can make the difference in changing jobs or moving up.

CHAPTER 4: GETTING THE JOB—RÉSUMÉS AND INTERVIEWING

In the fourth chapter, you'll learn where to look to find job openings for financial managers, or jobs that can lead to becoming a financial manager. You'll learn about how to put together a résumé and write a cover letter. Then it's on to the skills you need to ace the interview and, finally, some tips on keeping that job until you're ready to move up to the next one.

Expert Advice

Throughout the book you'll find interviews with financial managers working in a wide variety of roles, all at different stages of their careers. They have had some fascinating experiences and have great advice and tips for anyone looking to enter this field. There's a financial center manager for a credit union who worked his way up from the mailroom. There's a risk manager for a town in New England, who began his career in fire safety. A credit manager helps her bank decide where to lend their money by assessing financial reports from potential borrowers. Another manages insurance risk and policies for a national construction company. And a chief financial officer talks about her path to the top.

Every chapter contains stories like these—be sure to read them all!

We do not get to choose how we start out in life. We do not get to choose the day we are born or the family we are born into, what we are named at birth, what country we are born in, and we do not get to choose our ancestry. All these things are predetermined by a higher power. By the time you are old enough to start making decisions for yourself, a lot of things in your life are already in place. It's important, therefore, that you focus on the future, the only thing that you can change.—Idowu Koyenikan[1]

Where Do You Start?

As a financial manager, you have many opportunities. Take the first step toward your future!

Taking the first step is up to you! *Evelien Doosje/iStock/Getty Images*

Why Choose a Career as a Financial Manager?

What Is a Financial Manager?

*F*inancial managers are businesspeople who are responsible for the financial well-being of the institutions they work for, including companies, municipalities, universities, or other institutions. Together with their team members, financial managers analyze, understand, and report on everything to do with the finances of their institution. They also help others understand what all those numbers and statistics mean.

Financial managers are responsible for the financial well-being of their organizations.
Hiraman/E+/Getty Images

Financial managers need to understand how to prepare financial statements and other business reports, how to analyze and use financial data, and how to predict and recommend ways to maximize profit and expand opportunities for their institutions. Financial managers also need to understand things that relate to their particular industry, including regulations, tax and other laws, and specific financial practices. As the Bureau of Labor Statistics (BLS) points out, "Government financial managers must be experts on appropriations and budgeting processes; healthcare financial managers must understand billing, reimbursement, and other business matters related to healthcare."[1]

Financial managers are very important to the long-term health of their institutions. If finances are well managed, the company will be more profitable and more likely to continue in business for a long time. That means that it can employ more people, provide better benefits, and attract long-term investors with sustainably increasing share prices. For a nonprofit institution like a university or hospital, it means it can meet its goals and fulfill its mission, as well as attracting large donations. For a city or town, it means spending less taxpayer money on interest payments for debt and more on infrastructure and safety.

Financial managers may advance up the career ladder into executive positions, for example, chief financial officer (CFO) or even chief executive officer (CEO). A financial manager with the right credentials might also run his own business as a certified public accountant (CPA) or an attorney specializing in such areas as business/corporate law, tax law, estate planning, or forensic accounting.

> When money realizes that it is in good hands, it wants to stay and multiply in those hands.—Idowu Koyenikan[2]

What Does It Take to Be a Financial Manager?

As a financial manager, you'll need skills, knowledge, and personal qualities to do the job, as well as the right credentials for the type of financial management you plan to do.

KNOWLEDGE

- Accounting processes and norms
- Advanced math (especially algebra and statistics)
- Analyzing financial data
- Forecasting future earnings and expenses
- Legal knowledge relating to finance, contracts, compliance, and so forth
- Software related to statistical modeling, spreadsheets, and so forth

SKILLS AND PERSONAL QUALITIES

- Analytical skills to evaluate data and other information to help executives make decisions
- Communication skills to explain to others complex financial transactions, findings, projections, and statements
- Detail orientation to ensure that reports and analyses are complete and free from errors
- Organizational skills to maintain complex systems
- Leadership and interpersonal skills to work with teams
- Problem-solving skills
- Ability to work independently and with others

Finance managers work with individuals or as part of a team and generally bring a strong foundation of leading finance teams. Managers know how to enhance efficiency and productivity while maintaining confidence in their ability to move the company forward. Effective leaders demonstrate the ability to direct others and delegate tasks. Good financial managers take charge of situations and form effective solutions to encourage trust in their leadership skills.—Indeed.com Career Guide[3]

Financial managers hold positions of trust, so honesty and integrity are especially important. *Warchi/ iStock/Getty Images*

How Healthy Is the Job Market for Financial Managers?

The job market for all kinds of financial managers is very healthy and getting healthier every day. In 2020, *U.S. News & World Report* listed financial manager as number 27 on its list of one hundred best jobs, number 16 on its list of best paying jobs, and number 5 on its list of best business jobs. The highest financial manager salaries were in these top five industries:

- Professional, scientific, and technical services
- Management of companies and enterprises
- Manufacturing
- Finance and insurance
- Government[4]

What Are Job Prospects Like?

The BLS predicts that between 2019 and 2029, jobs for financial managers will grow much faster than other careers—about 15 percent overall. Of course, different industries will need different numbers of financial managers, so those numbers will vary depending on where you work. They predict more than fifty-nine thousand openings for financial managers each year in that decade. Those with master's degrees or certification in accounting and finance will be most in demand, as will cash managers, credit managers, and risk managers.

Not surprisingly, the states that employ the most financial managers are the ones with big cities: California, Texas, New York, Illinois, and Massachusetts. The states with greatest concentration of financial managers for their population compared to the nation as a whole (the location quotient) are Connecticut, Washington, D.C., Massachusetts, Illinois, and New Hampshire.[5]

Most financial managers start off in entry-level positions and work their way up to this more responsible role.

What Do Financial Managers Earn?

As a financial manager, you can expect to earn a very good living as soon as you enter this career. The BLS reports that as of September 2020, the median salary for financial managers was just under $130,000 per year. (Median means half of financial managers make more than that and half make less.) The lowest 10 percent made more than $68,000, and the highest 10 percent earned more than $200,000 annually.[6]

As a top executive, for instance, CFO, you would naturally earn a higher salary. How much that would be depends a lot on the kind of institution you work for and its goals, mission, size, and financial condition.

Where Do Financial Managers Work?

Financial managers work in office environments. They oversee their teams and work with top executives, so they interact with a lot of people on a regular basis as well as crunching all the numbers. Many financial managers work in large cities like New York, Chicago, or Los Angeles. But throughout North America are institutions of all types and sizes, so you might find the job you want in almost any location.

Financial managers usually work full time (forty hours per week) and may need to work more than that. Financial managers are usually considered "exempt employees," which means that this extra work is considered normal and covered by their salaries rather than being paid as overtime.

U.S. News & World Report rated financial management as high in upward mobility (opportunity for advancement), high in stress level (work environment and complexity), and average in flexibility (such things as work–life balance and alternative working schedules).

What Credentials Do Financial Managers Need?

To become a financial manager, you'll usually need to start with a bachelor's degree in a field like finance, accounting, economics, or business administration. It's getting more common for employers to expect financial managers to have a master's degree in one of those fields, too. So, if you happen to have a degree in something else and want to change fields, a master's degree can help you do that.

Certain kinds of financial manager jobs also require licenses and/or certifications. They are listed in the next section, which talks about different kinds of careers for financial managers.

Before becoming a financial manager, you'll most likely need to have five or more years of experience in a related business or financial job. This could include working as an accountant, a loan officer, a financial analyst, a securities sales agent, or something similar.

MIND THE GAAP

In the financial world, you come across the acronym GAAP a lot. What does it mean? GAAP stands for generally accepted accounting principles. GAAP is a set of rules that covers the "details, complexities, and legalities of business and corporate accounting."[7] In the United States, businesses that release financial statements to the public and companies that publicly trade their stock are legally required to conform to GAAP guidelines.

The key GAAP concepts include these principles:

- **Principle of regularity:** Strict adherence to established GAAP rules and regulations
- **Principle of consistency:** Standards applied consistently throughout the financial reporting process and across reporting periods
- **Principle of sincerity:** An accurate and impartial accounting of the company's finances
- **Principle of permanence of methods:** Consistent procedures are used across all financial reports
- **Principle of noncompensation:** Full reporting of all aspects of an organization's performance—positive or negative—without expectation or prospect of debt compensation
- **Principle of prudence:** Financial data reported based on facts, not speculation
- **Principle of continuity:** Assumption that the business will continue to operate when valuing assets
- **Principle of periodicity:** Revenue reporting follows standard accounting time periods, for example, fiscal quarters or fiscal years
- **Principle of materiality:** Reports contain full disclosure of all financial data and accounting information
- **Principle of utmost good faith:** All involved parties are assumed to be acting honestly (from the Latin expression *uberrimae fidei*)

Different Jobs for Financial Managers

There are many different types of financial manager. They may have different titles and cover different aspects of an institution's financial health, but they all have similar backgrounds and team leadership responsibilities. Here are a few of the options that can be found under that umbrella term "financial manager."

BANK MANAGER

A bank manager is a financial executive who oversees a bank or a branch office of a bank or other financial institution, for instance, a credit union. The job is to lead the team of banking staff members, ensure that the bank provides a high level of service and that the bank or branch is financially successful. A bank or branch manager's responsibilities include everything that happens at the bank, for example, hiring and training staff, managing resources, working with customer accounts, approving loans and lines of credit, setting and meeting sales goals, and growing business by developing and marketing new products and services, networking, and interacting with clients.

Bank managers need an educational background in finance or accounting, just like other financial managers. They also need experience and proven leadership skills. It's essential that bank or branch managers know the banking industry inside and out, and that they can actually perform all the functions that happen in the bank. They might need to audit the tellers' cash drawer, monitor deposits, approve or disapprove loans, file reports, keep up with audits and regulations, and communicate with customers, staff, and higher-level executives at the main office.

Branch managers, in particular, also need to be visible in the community, to build rapport with customers and attract new business. So, communications skills and people skills are especially important for someone in this role. To learn more about this job, read the interview with Lole Nuñez in chapter 2.

> A financial institution's executives place great confidence in the company's branch managers, expecting them to run their locations as their own businesses. A branch manager's job description includes assuming responsibility for virtually all functions of their branch—including growing that location's customer base and elevating the community's perception of the company's brand.—Will Kenton[8]

Bank and branch managers need financial knowledge and great people skills. *Vm/E+/Getty Images*

CASH MANAGER

Cash managers are responsible for monitoring and controlling the flow of money into and out of their organization. They supervise the flow of cash in and out of the business (called receipt and disbursement of cash) to meet their institution's investment and business needs. For instance, cash managers must project such things as when the institution will have too much or too little cash. Cash managers are needed in many different kinds of industries, from health care to manufacturing to financial services. Some of the duties of the cash manager include overseeing the allocation of cash balances (the amount of cash on hand), loans, cash disbursement (cash going out), and investments. They look for shortages and overages and ensure that these are corrected. Many state financial laws relate to cash, and the cash manager makes sure the institution is in compliance.

Cash managers work both independently and as part of the team, often overseeing the work of junior personnel in the department and providing training. Most cash managers have bachelor's degrees, and about 25 percent also have master's degrees.[9] You'll need between four and seven years of previous experience to be promoted to a cash manager position. Other titles for this position include "cash allocation and forecasting manager" and "treasury cash senior analyst."

CHIEF FINANCIAL OFFICER (CFO)

An institution's chief financial officer is part of the "C-suite" team of top executives. The CFO is responsible for managing the institution's financial actions, including analyzing strengths and weaknesses, financial planning, managing cash flow, and proposing corrections when they're needed. The CFO manages the finance and accounting departments, and is responsible for ensuring that all financial records are accurate and meet all required deadlines. The CFO is also responsible for making sure that the institution's financial practices meet all the legal requirements set by the Securities and Exchange Commission (SEC) and other regulatory bodies, as well as following generally accepted accounting principles.

The CFO reports directly to the chief executive officer (CEO). This is a position of the greatest responsibility because the CFO plays a significant role in determining what the institution's financial decisions and actions will be. The CFO also works with other managers across every department.

The CFO is the highest-ranking position in the financial industry and the third-highest-ranking position in other kinds of institutions, behind the CEO and the chief operating officer (COO). This position is sometimes called "finance officer" or "treasurer." In nonprofit organizations, the treasurer is usually a volunteer member of the board of directors; in a large nonprofit, there might be a finance committee chaired by the treasurer. Don't miss the interview at the end of this chapter with La Vonda Williams, CFO for two exciting start-up companies in the health field in New York City.

It is often said that when a non-financially-minded person sees numbers, numbers are all that person sees. But when a financially-minded person sees numbers, that person sees the story behind the numbers.—Dave Robinson[10]

COMPLIANCE MANAGER

Compliance managers work to ensure that their organization is correctly following all federal, state, and industry standards, rules, and regulation. This can include ethical standards, tax laws, accounting standards, and all the various legal rules and regulations that are put in place to protect both companies and their clients. Compliance managers work in many kinds of institutions, including banks and other financial institutions.

To be successful as a compliance manager takes a strong sense of integrity and the ability to stand up in a professional way to others in the company, including executives who may outrank you. It's the compliance manager's role to point out when things aren't being done correctly, when ethical or legal corners are being cut, or when wrongdoing has occurred. The compliance manager is responsible for notifying regulatory or enforcement agencies when an issue needs investigation. Not everyone appreciates this kind of oversight, so it's important for a compliance manager to have a thick skin and a willingness to stand up for what is right even in the face of opposition.

Strong attention to detail is essential in this role, along with in-depth knowledge of relevant laws and regulations. Compliance managers build their knowledge and skills by gaining experience as compliance analysts. It's a hard job, but compliance managers report very high levels of job satisfaction. Many compliance managers hold bachelor's degrees in nonfinancial fields, for instance, political science, psychology, or business administration.[11]

Because the job of a compliance manager is to ensure the organization complies with rules and regulations, it's critical to have a strong moral compass and a track record of ethical decision-making. Of course, integrity is essential for everyone on a compliance team, but perhaps even more so for the compliance manager, who must direct analysts, compliance specialists and other staff members in making sound decisions.—Robert Half[12]

CONTROLLER

A controller (also known as a financial controller) is a senior executive who heads the accounting department and is responsible for an organization's accounting, payroll, accounts payable, and accounts receivable. Controllers help guide strategic financial decisions to ensure the company's financial health. Controllers prepare financial forecasts and reports (e.g., balance sheets, income statements, and future earnings/expenses analyses). They supervise their staff to maintain such accounting records as the general ledger, payroll, and taxes, as well as reconcile accounts, coordinate audits, and manage budgets. Controllers recommend financial performance benchmarks and ensure compliance for taxes and other regulations. The controller usually reports to the CFO in a larger institution; in a smaller company, the controller might be the highest-ranking financial officer.

Generally, a company's controller will have an MBA degree and at least seven years of accounting experience. Controllers often have specialized certification, for example, chartered public accountant (CPA), chartered global management accountant (CGMA), chartered financial analyst (CFA), or certified management accountant (CMA).[13]

> This is a great career for someone who always likes to learn something new. See if you can start with an internship or at the junior credit analyst level. That's a good stepping-stone if you want to try it on for size. You learn a lot. There's a lot thrown at you at once, but if you're a fast learner and have an aptitude for writing, math and accounting, you could find it's the right fit for you. Promotion along the track from junior analyst to credit analyst to senior analyst may be rapid or it may be slow depending on your skill and your employer.—Jill White, interview in chapter 3

CREDIT MANAGER

Credit managers are responsible for the team that analyzes and recommends actions regarding the credit side of an institution's business. This includes setting credit-rating standards, terms, and limits, as well as monitoring collections of past-due accounts. Credit managers for financial institutions evaluate proposals and financial records from businesses seeking credit or investment. They may work in banks or credit unions, or in accounting, mortgage, or credit card companies. Credit managers are also found in automobile dealerships, home renovation or contracting companies, retail outlets that extend credit to customers, and even in elective surgery practices.[14]

Credit managers need to keep up with the constantly changing practice of credit scoring, as well as understand the financial products that are available in financial services. Credit managers in banks, for instance, work directly with customers to evaluate and recommend whether to extend them credit, so good interpersonal skills are essential. The required education for credit managers varies depending on the size of the organization. A bachelor's degree in finance is the first step; larger institutions usually also want to see an MBA on a credit manager's résumé.

As credit manager Jillian White says, "Analysis is the nitty gritty—the core of what we do. Being a good analyst means you're able to interpret the numbers and put it into a format where someone who doesn't have a background in that specific business could easily pick up the presentation and say, 'I understand what's going on.'" Be sure to read her interview at the end of chapter 3 for her expert insight into the work of a credit manager and her department.

People skills are very important for credit managers, who figure out which people and projects should be considered for loans. *Skynesher/E+/Getty Images*

FUND MANAGER

Fund managers oversee such financial investments as mutual funds, pension funds, trust funds, or hedge funds. A good fund manager aims to produce consistent, long-term performance in the fund.

The fund manager's responsibility is to implement the fund's investment strategy through trading activities. Fund managers manage teams of investment analysts, who evaluate financial and investment information to recommend when to buy, sell, or hold the securities in their fund. Fund managers research companies, study and understand what's going on in economy and the financial industry, as well as relevant trends. They must be knowledgeable about stocks, bonds, and other types of securities, then choose the ones that best fit the fund's strategy and decide when to buy and when to sell. Fund managers also write reports for clients and potential clients, explaining how the fund is doing and its risks and strategies.[15]

Fund managers must have lots of experience as well as appropriate degrees (usually including an MBA or other financial master's degree) and professional credentials. Many start as research analysts and then become portfolio managers. Many fund managers are chartered financial analysts (CFA), which requires rigorous investment analysis and portfolio management coursework. Some fund managers have been so successful that they actually became famous, for instance, Peter Lynch (manager of Fidelity Investments' Magellan Fund from 1977 to 1990) and Albert Nicholas (founder of the Nicholas Company).

INTERNATIONAL FINANCE MANAGER

International finance managers work in many types of industries, for example, international banks and companies. They develop financial and accounting systems, prepare financial reports, set and pursue financial goals, and manage the organization's finances.

International finance managers must understand the relevant financial theories, strategies, and regulations affecting foreign investments. This understanding generally begins with a bachelor's degree in finance, accounting, or economics, often specifically in international finance. An MBA or other relevant master's degree is usually expected as well. Many employers prefer international finance managers to hold a CPA license and/or the international equivalent. It can be very useful to know more than one language to work as an international finance manager.

Ratings analysts evaluate the ability of companies or governments to pay their debts, including bonds. On the basis of their evaluation, a management team rates the risk of a company or government not being able to repay its bonds.

INSURANCE MANAGER

There are two kinds of insurance managers. One kind manages operations for a small insurance company or for a branch office of a larger insurance company. This type of insurance manager supervises the insurance office staff and sales force, maintains client records, and keeps track of policy sales and commissions. The insurance manager's job is to be sure that all rules and regulations are being followed, that client records are filed promptly and accurately, and that actuary data and information are being used to evaluate sales to and claims from the company's clients.

The other kind of insurance manager is generally a type of risk manager (see risk manager, next). The insurance manager oversees the organization's insurance programs. Risk managers analyze such things as exposure to risk, and they analyze and classify risks to be sure that the right insurance coverage is in place. Insurance managers collect data, generate reports and models to show where insurance is needed, and evaluate and recommend insurance products to the company. They also manage self-insured company plans.

Insurance risk managers generally have at least a bachelor's degree, along with several years of experience in a related area and some supervisory experience as well. It's important to know and understand the activities of the entire company to plan for any risks that may need to be covered. Kevin Ward talks about his experience as an insurance manager for a national construction company in chapter 4.

Risk managers need to know the many places risk can come from and how to protect their organization. *Blue Planet Studio/iStock/Getty Images*

RISK MANAGER

Risk managers develop strategies to reduce their organization's chance of financial loss or exposure that could come from many different directions. Financial risk can come from business operations, financial transactions, investment strategies, and currency or commodity price changes. A risk manager uses various financial tools and techniques to manage certain kinds of financial risks; for instance, in a bank, the risk manager's job would be to balance activities to be sure that interest rates were managed properly, because fluctuating interest rates create a major risk for banks.

Another kind of financial risk can come from physical risk, for instance, insurance claims that arise from accidents or unsafe conditions. In chapter 4, Marty Maynard, risk manager for the town of Windsor, Connecticut, gives his insights into the complex role of managing risk for a municipality.

Risk managers create overall risk management strategies, perform risk assessments and evaluations, communicate levels of risk and necessary responses (e.g., appropriate insurance) to decision makers in their institutions, review contracts, implement health and safety protocols, and maintain records of insurance policies and claims.

Traditional risk management, sometimes called "insurance risk management," has focused on "pure risks" (i.e., possible loss by fortuitous or accidental means) but not business risks (i.e., those that may present the possibility of loss or gain). Financial institutions also employ a different type of risk management, which focuses on the effects of financial risks on the organization. For example, interest rate risk is a bank's most important financial risk, and various hedging tools and techniques such as derivatives are used to manage banks' exposure to interest rate volatility.—IRMI[16]

MORE FINANCE-RELATED CAREERS

Many more careers are related to finance and accounting. Here's a quick look at some related financial jobs:

ACCOUNTANTS

Accountants maintain and interpret financial records. There are many kinds of accountants:

- Government accountants work for government agencies. They audit private businesses and individuals who are subject to government regulations or taxation. They make sure that revenues are received and spent according to current laws and regulations.
- Management accountants (also called cost, managerial, industrial, corporate, or private accountants) record and analyze financial information for use by the institutions they work for, rather than the general public. They may help plan the cost of doing business or work with financial managers on such things as asset management.
- Public accountants cover many kinds of accounting, auditing, tax, and consulting. Their clients include corporations, governments, and individuals. They work with financial documents that clients are legally required to disclose. Some advise corporations about the tax advantages of certain business decisions; others prepare individual income tax returns.

- Certified public accountants (CPAs) are public accountants, often having their own businesses or working for public accounting firms. Publicly traded companies are required to have CPAs sign documents being submitted to the Securities and Exchange Commission (SEC), for instance, annual and quarterly reports.
- Forensic accountants are public accountants who investigate financial crimes (e.g., securities fraud and embezzlement, bankruptcies and contract disputes) and complex and potentially criminal financial transactions. Forensic accountants know accounting and finance as well as law and investigative techniques. Many work closely with law enforcement and lawyers during investigations and are called as expert witnesses.

ANALYSTS

Financial analysts are part of the financial management team. You might start as an analyst and work your way up to financial manager. For instance:

- Ratings analysts evaluate whether companies or governments are able to pay their debts. Their evaluation helps the management team rate the risk associated with company or government bonds.
- Risk analysts evaluate the risk associated with certain investment decisions to manage unpredictability and limit potential losses. They consider investment recommendations involving stocks, bonds, and mutual funds in a portfolio.

AUDITORS

- External auditors come from outside an organization to review clients' financial statements, identify problems or issues, and report to investors and authorities as to whether the statements have been correctly prepared and reported.
- Internal auditors identify and prevent mismanagement of funds in the institutions they work for. They find ways to help stop waste and prevent fraud.
- IT auditors are internal auditors who analyze and assess their company's technological infrastructure. They ensure that systems are accurate and efficient, as well as secure and in compliance with regulations.

The Pros and Cons of Being a Financial Manager

Being a financial manager is a great career. What are the pros and cons? That depends a lot on what's important to you. Take a look at the qualities that go along with being a financial manager and see which ones you think are "pros" and which ones you think are "cons":

- The job outlook is very good for financial managers. BLS predictions include 15 percent job grown between 2019 and 2029, much faster than average.[17]
- The need for financial managers varies by industry and by institution size.
- Risk manager is the type of financial manager that will be most needed.
- Financial manager jobs pay well, with the median wage being more than $120,000 per year.
- You'll need a college degree and probably an advanced degree.
- You may need additional licenses or certifications, depending on the type of financial manager you want to be.
- You'll need years of experience in finance-related jobs to be promoted to financial manager.
- You'll be leading a team.
- You're likely to have good job security.
- You'll be working indoors, in an office environment.
- Financial management can be stressful, with a lot of responsibility for detail and deadlines.
- Financial managers are responsible for many aspects of their institution's financial health, including reducing costs, increasing income, and managing risk.
- This is complex, data-driven, mathematically oriented work where it's important to be accurate and not make mistakes.
- You may work longer than forty hours per week, especially when report or tax deadlines are looming.
- You could work in almost any location, for a large or small company, nonprofit, municipality, or other organization.

As a financial manager, you make sure that all is well with your organization's financial health and well-being. *NicoElNino/iStock/Getty Images*

Summary

With so many different kinds of financial manager careers out there, you have many possible options if you're interested in doing this kind of work. Starting with very similar educational backgrounds, one person might become a credit manager for a bank, another might evaluate risk for a large corporation, someone else might be the manager of a bank branch, another could be the controller of a company. You could focus on the needs of your own town or grapple with the complexities of international finance. It's all up to you!

In the next chapter, we'll talk about how to make your career plan so you can figure out if being a financial manager is right for you and what steps you'll want to take to reach your ultimate goal. Every financial manager knows that data is important—and that's what will go into your plan in Step 2: Forming a Career Plan.

LA VONDA WILLIAMS, CHIEF FINANCIAL OFFICER

La Vonda Williams is chief financial officer (CFO) for Onegevity Health LLC and NutriTiva LLC, two early-stage companies in New York City. She holds an SB in mechanical and materials science and engineering from Harvard and an MBA from Stanford Graduate School of Business. She is an experienced leader, having worked in positions of increasing responsibility in Fortune 500 companies, government, and start-ups. Her expertise is in building operational entities from ideas, implementing financial product strategies, financial risk management, increasing team efficiency, and cultivating organizational culture. She is also a member of CHIEF, "a private network built to drive more women into positions of power and keep them there."

La Vonda Williams. *Courtesy of Zachary Tyler Newton*

What is the role of a chief financial officer?

The chief financial officer is responsible for the full financial health of a company, so every aspect of the company's financial well-being. That includes all of the company's activities that have a financial impact, whether it's growth, acquisition, financial reporting, tax filings. In many cases, it includes all kinds of insurance—seeing that risks are managed—as well as expense and financial policies across the teams, forecasting, sales projections. We're involved in raising and allocating financial resources across the business. So, it really gives you an opportunity to get involved in and impact all the different aspects of the business. You have a lot of reach into every area for a smaller company; with a larger company, you have a team that handles that for you. But in a small company, it's all aspects of the life cycle and growth cycle of the company. All those things become relevant at different stages of a company. It can be a lot of fun!

How did you become a chief financial officer?

I'd say it was a situation where experience met with opportunity. Someone referred me for this role based on their knowledge of my background. I spent a lot of time working in financial markets and financial firms. I love start-ups. I'd worked as a C-level employee at a start-up before. I'm CFO for two companies. Because they're early-stage startups, it makes it possible for me to handle both of them. Onegevity Health LLC is a health intelligence company that works on the test–teach–treat model, providing health and wellness recommendations based on various test outcomes, for example, the gut biome. It's really a company that uses a lot of science and research to provide consumer health information, but it also partners with large pharmaceutical and consumer packaged goods firms that rely on our proprietary research for drug repurposing or product formulation studies. The other company, NutriTiva LLC, is a direct-to-consumer product company that provides highly nutritious functional beverage disks that are dissolvable in water and, therefore, are also low-waste and portable. It's high-quality nutrients and supplements without all the packaging. It will have a greatly reduced impact on the environment compared to other beverages.

What is a typical day on your job?

There's a combination of executive meetings, cash management, and fielding lots of e-mails from our vendors, suppliers, investors, and partners. I work with our accounting team and tax team to be sure our reporting is on track, our payments are being scheduled, and incoming cash receipts are not delayed. As an early-stage company CFO, I do many tasks myself directly. I also spend time reading, reviewing, and revising the economic terms of our contracts when we're negotiating with our clients and vendors to be sure we're strategic about our pricing, and there are no hidden costs we're not considering. Regular reporting to our CEO is a critical function that informs his business decision-making. All the C-level team members work very closely together so we come up with the best solution for any given scenario. It's very collaborative.

What's the best part of being a chief financial officer?

You interact with all the different aspects of the business, because every major business function has some kind of top-line or bottom-line impact. I work with research at times, sales at times, marketing at times. I work with our investors. If you love business, as I do, financial performance is like the score card for your business, the thermometer for your business—you can see how healthy your company is. There are so many ways that the decisions you make on a day-to-day basis impact the financial performance. If I were siloed in one area, I'd probably be bored. Because I'm involved in so many aspects of the business, it keeps it fun and exciting. I also have an opportunity to teach. It's part of my personality to coach, to teach, so I spend a lot of time explaining to team members why we can or can't do things, making sure our capital lasts as long as possible, that our margins or revenues are as strong as possible. Not every function in a company is always focused on that commercial challenge, so it's also part of my job to be sure every part of the company understands to be frugal, to be prudent, not to burn through our capital. Being a constant reminder of our goal to get the plane off the tarmac and into the air before we are out of runway—that's my job.

What's the most challenging part of being a chief financial officer?

Exactly the same thing that makes it fun makes it challenging. You want to keep your eye on everything, and you have to decide what's most critical. You need to understand the economic, legal, regulatory, and tax implications of every decision you make. You have to be efficient with your time. You want to catch every penny, every nuance, but also keep your eye on the big picture. If an error is made, I have to catch it. To see the big picture, you have to rely on your team for the details versus doing everything yourself. That's probably true for every executive role, but it's certainly true when you need every penny to balance.

What's the most surprising thing about being a chief financial officer?

The impression I always had was that you had to be a CPA to be a good CFO— that people only wanted accountants to be CFOs. I wondered if my background would align. But I soon discovered "You've got this." So many skills are involved in being a CFO, but this job needs someone who can communicate across the company, understand the life cycle of the company. You have to be tactful in telling senior people "no" sometimes. Having a strong background in capital markets is something I took for granted, but it turned out to be very helpful—understanding markets for bonds, stocks, and derivatives products. I knew a lot more than I thought I did. So, I was surprised at how all my other skills, even my contract negotiations, all played a part in being good at this role. You may not realize all the beneficial skills you have, but perspective and insight have great value.

How did (or didn't) your education prepare you to be a chief financial officer?

My undergraduate degree is in engineering, so I have a comfort with numbers and quantitative analysis of all kinds—all that was useful. In terms of graduate school, business—period. Focusing on entrepreneurship, understanding what companies need at every stage, the different kinds of risk. Going to business school was very important for that, and studying both failed and successful company strategies was priceless. I've worked in firms with very strong risk management cultures, which was very helpful. You have to keep your eye on risk, predicting it, managing it, preparing for it. Risk can show up anywhere. You have to consider everything. Both formal and informal education prepared me—soft skills and hard skills.

Is being a chief financial officer what you expected?

In many ways, yes. But it varies by company and by culture. So, in some ways, I had no expectations, because I know that for early-stage companies and middle-sized companies, cultures vary a lot based on the management team. How much people expect of you, rely on you—that's a function of you and how you relate to them. It's more fun and more intellectually challenging than I expected. And I love the people I work with. If you enjoy solving puzzles of any kind, business in general and being CFO in particular is very much like fitting pieces of a puzzle together.

What's next? Where do you see yourself going from here?

That's a tough one! For me, I love early- to late-stage small private companies and middle-sized companies, so I could see myself staying in the C-suite, maybe being a chief operating officer (which I've done before) or chief executive officer. Also, joining corporate boards is an aspiration, because they're often looking for people who can understand the financial reports and sit on or chair audit committees. I would be interested in a late-stage, pre-IPO private company or a public company board. Many corporate boards value the experience of launching viable businesses from their idea stage to profitability, so I'm looking forward to bringing all these skills to bear. My current responsibility of reporting to our company directors also offers a training ground for future board service. Those could be private or public company boards.

Where do you see the role of chief financial officer going in the future?

I think it's always been a role where trust, integrity, judgment, and discretion are required and valued, so that will never change. As with most things, as our economy and culture have become more open and exposed, with more outward facing communication to the public, the presentation skill set is very important, and outreach through social media is becoming more prevalent. Communicating with the public and throughout an organization is part of company branding, company marketing, and I think CFOs will become more involved in that. Similarly, the news and information cycle has shortened considerably through the adoption of digital media. Whereas corporate budgeting, forecasting, and announcements used to be more static, now we see and will continue to see forecasting being dynamic and ongoing. This will require CFOs to be nimbler.

What is your advice for a young person aspiring to be a chief financial officer?

There are many paths to get there, but I'd certainly say, it makes it easier if you've had exposure to some of the larger financial firms in the industry—investment banks, private equity companies, middle market lenders. Getting exposure to business operations and finances on the grand scale is very helpful. It's easier to move to a smaller company with years of experience from a larger, reputable one. Once people see that you've developed a skill in a tried-and-true platform, you'll get more opportunities to use those skills in other settings. I'd advise following a traditional route at first, and then get creative. I've seen a lot of people make that move in that direction. And if you have an interest in accounting, by all means, study accounting, but that's not the only path. You don't necessarily need a degree in accounting. You must have certain fundamental skill sets, feathers in your cap, tools in your belt, and after that you can be super-creative with your career.

2

Forming a Career Plan

Planning the Plan

*N*ow that you've had an introduction to some of the many options for financial managers, what do you do next? When you're aiming for a career like financial manager, that requires a certain amount of both education and experience, it's even more important to plan ahead than it would be for an entry-level job. You need to have a good understanding of yourself. You also need to understand the career itself. If you put that information together in an organized way, it can help guide your decision-making as you prepare to become a financial manager.

Advance planning is the key to your future career. *Miodrag ignjatovic/E+/Getty Images*

STARTING AT THE BEGINNING?

If you're still in high school and planning for college, or if you're in college and planning your next move, then you're starting at the beginning. This is a great place to be because you can chart your path from your very first step.

MOVING UP?

If you're already working, and you'd like to move into financial management, that's also a great place to be! You're in a position to see how the business works, get to know people in many departments, and connect with mentors and colleagues who can give you tips on advancing in your career.

CHANGING JOBS?

If you're already in a job that doesn't have an opportunity for you to move into a financial manager role, you may be considering finding a different employer. In that case, this is a great time to do some digging and some advance planning to find out what you need to know and what you need to do to position yourself to successfully make a move.

Where to Begin

1. First, you need to think about yourself—what you like and don't like, what you're good at and not so good at, and what feels like a comfortable fit for you.
2. Next, you need to find some information—this can come from all kinds of sources, for example, books, internet searches, and people you know or who work in your community. You can start with the "Further Resources" at the back of this book!
3. Then, you need to know what you need to know: How do you get ready to pursue a career as a financial manager? What can you do while you're still in high school?

4. What kind of education will you need? What kind of training will you need? And how do you go about getting it? See chapter 3 for more about the education path.

5. Remember that the best plans are flexible!

Figuring Yourself Out

Every good career plan begins with you. A good place to start is by thinking about your own qualities. What are *you* like? Where do *you* feel comfortable, and where do *you* feel uncomfortable?

Let's start by making a few lists. Ask yourself the questions in the box called "All About You" and then think about how your answers match up with a career as a financial manager.

ALL ABOUT YOU

PERSONALITY TRAITS

- Are you introverted or extroverted?
- How do you react to stress—do you stay calm when others panic?
- Do you prefer interacting with people or working closely with technology?
- Are you respectful to others?
- Are you polite?
- How much money do you want to make—just enough or all of it?
- What does the word "success" mean to you?

INTERESTS

- Are you interested in how systems work?
- Are you interested in solving problems?
- Are you interested in helping people?
- Are you interested in moving up a clear career ladder?
- Or would you like to move around from one kind of job to another?

LIKES AND DISLIKES

- Do you like to figure things out or to know ahead of time exactly what's coming up?
- Do you like working on your own or as part of a team?
- Do you like talking to people, or do you prefer minimal interaction?
- Can you take direction from a boss or teacher, or do you want to decide for yourself how to do things?
- Do you like things to be the same or to change a lot?

STRENGTHS AND CHALLENGES

- What is something you accomplished that you're proud of?
- Are you naturally good at school, or do you have to work harder at some subjects?
- Are you flexible and able to adapt to changes and new situations?
- Are you good at numbers?
- Are you a good communicator?
- Are you good at remembering and following complex directions and rules?
- Can you manage your own time, or do you do better when you're meeting a boss's or teacher's expectations?
- What is your best trait (in your opinion)?
- What is your worst trait (in your opinion)?

Remember, this list is for you. Be as honest as you can—tell yourself the truth, not what you think someone else would want the answer to be. Once you have a good list of your own interests, strengths, challenges, likes and dislikes, you'll be in a good position to know what kind of career you want.

Now it's time to think about the characteristics of the different possible jobs you might do. Think about the location of the jobs and what kind of place you want to work in. Take a look at the questions in the box called "About the Job" and consider what you'd like your career to be like.

Take a little time to wonder about yourself and your future—then you'll be ready to plan.
FangXiaNuo/E+/Getty Images

ABOUT THE JOB

- What kind of work will you be doing?
- What kind of environment will you be working in?
- Will you have regular 9 to 5 hours, or will you be working evenings and/or weekends?
- What kind of community do you want to live in—city, suburb, or small town?
- Will you be able to live where you want to? What career compromises might be necessary if you choose location as a top priority?
- Or will you need to go where the job is? What lifestyle compromises might be necessary if you choose a particular type of job as a top priority?
- Will you work directly with customers?
- Will you have a boss or be a boss?
- How much education will you need?
- Do you also need certification?
- Is there room for advancement?

- What does the job pay?
- What kind of benefits will the employer provide?
- Is there room to change jobs and try different things within the same organization?

Finally, what does your gut say? Listen to the little voice in the back of your mind that says, "That's the one for me!" or "No way!" You already know what you'll like and what you'll be good at. A good fit is very important—more important than salary or many other considerations. So think it through with your head—but also listen to your heart.

Am I Right for a Career as a Financial Manager?

Certain qualities help make a successful financial manager that go beyond the basics of education and work experience.

Trained to see the bigger picture, the top finance and accounting professionals tend to look at their jobs and careers from a more holistic perspective. The best people in finance understand that to succeed, they must aid and encourage success in others. They are sharp, analytical thinkers, but also strong communicators who can share their insights when they are called upon. The best people in finance are the types to explore opportunities for continuous improvement and can prioritize and formulate solutions that create win-win situations.—Clarity Recruitment[1]

The following list covers qualities that experts[2] have identified as important to success for financial managers. That means potential employers will want to know which of these attributes apply to you.

Notice how the list includes both "hard skills" like math knowledge and technical proficiency, as well as such "soft skills" as communication and emotional intelligence. In fact, although this list is in alphabetical order, here's a little secret: All the experts put "leadership" at the top of their own lists.

- Ability to work independently
- Ability to work with others
- Adaptability and resilience
- Analytical skills
- Attention to detail
- Communication skills
- Detail oriented
- Emotional intelligence
- Empathy
- Enterprising
- Growth mindset
- Improvement-focused
- Insight
- Intellectual curiosity
- Interpersonal skills
- Leadership
- Mathematical proficiency
- Organizational skills
- Persistence
- Positivity
- Prioritization
- Problem solving
- Sense of humor
- Solutions-oriented
- Technological skills
- Vision

Where to Go for Help

The internet has so much information—about jobs and everything else—that it can be hard to separate the good data from the noise. So, let's take a look at how to find good information about financial manager careers.

START WHERE YOU ARE

If you're in high school, you have a great resource when it comes to planning your future—your guidance counselor. Your guidance counselor's job is to give you *guidance* about your plans beyond graduation. Drop by the guidance office and ask for help. They have lots of resources—including books like this one—that can point you in the direction you're looking for.

Other great people to talk to while you're in school are the teachers who cover relevant subjects. Talk to your business teacher, your math teacher, your economics teacher—they may have some good insight or suggestions about where to learn more or who else to talk to.

TALK TO PROFESSIONALS IN YOUR COMMUNITY

Right now your town has professional financial managers and other finance professionals. If you or your family already know people who work in these fields, you've already taken the first step. If you don't, you can pick up the phone or walk into your local bank to find the professionals who can give you advice.

You may be able arrange an internship, a summer job, or even just a job-shadowing day, where you can learn about the organization and how it works in person. The world is full of financial managers who started just like this, for example, a bank compliance officer who had a summer job as a teller for a branch of that same bank while she was in high school or a young man who started in the mailroom of a bank and worked his way up to financial center manager for a credit union. You can read about that second story in detail in the interview with Lole Nuñez at the end of this chapter!

GO TO THE LIBRARY

Your local public library has tons of books about finance careers that you can find and read for free. Libraries are great! You can find so much more than books on the shelf. Librarians know how to help you find the information you need, and they genuinely enjoy helping you find it. If you haven't made a friend of your local librarian yet, it's never too late!

If you're in high school or college, you also have a school library or media center that will have books on all kinds of topics, including careers—and a school or academic librarian who is eager and willing to help you.

If you find a book you want to read and your library doesn't have it, the librarian may be able to get it for you through interlibrary loan. Just ask!

The library is a great source of information on careers and everything else. *SeventyFour/iStock/Getty Images*

SEARCH IT!

The internet is a very useful place to start your own research, as long as you're careful and particular about your sources. Sure, the internet is full of distracting memes and nonsense, but if you search carefully, you can find lots of information about every possible career.

One incredibly useful site is the Bureau of Labor Statistics Occupational Outlook Handbook (https://www.bls.gov/ooh/). This site has tons of information about almost every kind of job found in the United States. Each job category has extensive data, organized into such useful categories as "What They Do," "Work Environment," "Job Outlook," and other information. It even has a summary page that pulls out the most important points. It's written in simple, plain English that anyone can understand.

Another great source of information is job postings. Go to the sites that consolidate job postings, including Indeed.com, Linkedin.com, Careerbuilder. com, or Monster.com, and look for ads for financial managers. Pretend that you're already a job seeker and search for the kind of job you'd like to have. Read the ads to see what kind of educational background and experience real employers are looking for. These ads are usually quite detailed, which means they're a gold mine of information about these careers.

Making High School Count

If you are interested in becoming a financial manager or another financial career, be sure you're making the most of your high school education. Don't forget to talk to your teachers, as we just discussed. What else can you do to start preparing for a career as a financial manager while you're still in high school?

WHAT CLASSES SHOULD YOU TAKE?

Many high schools offer a wide array of relevant classes for students who want to go into business or financial careers. Of course, not every high school has all the classes listed here, so talk with your teachers about which classes at your school will be the most useful for you. You can also find online versions of certain high school classes, if you want to learn something that your school doesn't offer.

Here's a list of courses that can help you be ready for college if you plan to become a financial manager one day:

- Accounting
- Algebra I and II
- Business law
- Business management
- Composition
- E-commerce
- Economics

- International business
- Marketing
- Office procedures
- Public speaking
- Statistics[3]

DO WELL AND GRADUATE

That should go without saying, shouldn't it? But we'll say it anyway, because it's important. You're already thinking about the kind of future you want. You're looking into what you need to know and what you need to do to get there. Don't waste that effort! Work hard at your classes, do your best, and graduate!

ASK FOR HELP

Did you ever notice how in books or movies, right before the hero gets into a world of hurt, they always say to their friends, "I have to do this by myself"?

No one does anything successfully all by themselves. Human beings are social. We depend on each other. Everybody needs help at some point. You might need help understanding something in your homework. You might need help dealing with a difficult person. You might need help finding a job. You might need help figuring out which colleges to apply for. You might lock yourself out of your car. Whatever you need help with, someone else has already been through it and can help you get through it.

A lot of people are very willing to give help but don't feel like they can ask for help themselves. Don't be too proud or too afraid to ask for help when you need it. Needing help doesn't mean you're weak or incapable. It just means you're human.

GET SOME EXPERIENCE

You don't have to have job experience during your high school years to become a successful financial manager. But if you have or can find the opportunity, it's a great way to get to know the field. Jobs or internships also help fill out your

You can build your experience through an internship or part-time job even before you graduate.
Drazen/E+/Getty Images

résumé, which is good for college applications and, later on, job applications. (Résumés are covered in detail in chapter 4.)

Internships

Internships are generally unpaid work experience; sometimes you can arrange to get school credit for an internship. An internship should be an educational experience, not just making copies and getting coffee. It can be harder for a high-school student to find an internship, because internships are usually aimed at college students. A company has to jump through additional hoops when working with a minor, so some companies may not accept high-school students for internships. And if you decide to hold off on an internship until you're in college, that's just fine, too.

Taking an internship while you are in high school comes with trade-offs. To be sure your internship is worth the time you put into it, remember these important tips (adapted from an article in *U.S. News & World Report*):[4]

- **Know what you're looking for:** Focus on finding an internship that meets your goals.
- **Time is precious:** You'll need to devote about ten to fifteen hours each week to an internship. Be sure time spent on interning is balanced by maintaining your grades and your social and extracurricular activities.
- **Transportation:** How will you get there and back? If you have to spend a lot of money for transportation, think about how that balances out with what you're learning from the internship.
- **Start looking a few months ahead:** It takes time to research internships, interview for them, and work them into your busy schedule. Give yourself the time to do it right.
- **Approach people you know first:** People know other people. Let your teachers, coaches, parents, parents' friends, friends' parents, and your social media connections know that you're looking for an internship. They may know a good place or someone else who can help you find what you're looking for.
- **Search online:** Try such internship sites as InternshipPrograms.com or InternMatch.io to find internships in your area of interest and location. Google local businesses to see who you could talk to.
- **Have an elevator pitch ready:** This is just a short, thirty-second introduction to who you are and what you're looking for. You could say something like, "I'm [your name]. I'm a high-school junior, and I'm interested in finding an internship opportunity in banking. I've taken courses in business and economics, but I'm hoping to get some experience with a real company during the school year."
- **Overcome objections:** If the company you're interested in doesn't usually take on high-school interns, let them know what you have to offer. Everyone likes to know how they would benefit by doing something. Flexible schedule? Outgoing personality? Ideas for marketing to people your age?
- **Approach with caution:** Some internships are structured to take advantage of high-school students without providing them any real education or useful experience. Be sure the duties and responsibilities are spelled out clearly (in writing) for both you and the employer. Don't take on more hours than you can actually do—it's important to maintain your GPA and your social life! And be aware of people around you

who might not remember (or want) to treat you in an age-appropriate way—if you're ever uncomfortable, go directly to your supervisor (or their supervisor), your parents, a teacher, or another adult you trust.

Summer or Part-Time Jobs

Summer jobs or part-time jobs during the school year are also great ways to gain experience in the field, while earning some money at the same time. Here are some important tips to know about working while you're in high school.

- **Any job is a good job:** Almost any job you do while you're in high school will give you a chance to learn about how businesses work.
- **But—a relevant job is better:** If you already know for sure that financial management is where you want to end up eventually, it makes sense to look for a summer or part-time job that relates to that goal—for instance, working as a teller at a local bank or answering phones in an insurance or real-estate company.
- **How much time do you have?:** In the summer, you could work as much as forty hours a week—a regular full-time job. A part-time job during the school year needs to be balanced against your other obligations (school, sports, activities, friends, and family), so you should expect to work ten to twenty hours per week and no more.
- **Transportation:** How will you get to your job and back? Do you have a car? Is there a reliable bus system? Can someone take you and pick you up?
- **Start looking a few months ahead:** Just like an internship, it takes time to find and apply for a job, interview, and get started. You'll need plenty of time, especially if jobs are scarce in your location.
- **Approach people you know first:** As with internships, the people you know can introduce you to people they know. Let people know that you're looking for a job—especially the adults in your life. They may know who's looking for summer help or even need someone to help out in their own office.
- **Search online:** A simple internet search for "part-time jobs near me" or "summer jobs banking" will generate loads of results. Often, you can sort the results by how long it's been posted and how many miles from

your home. You can also find local companies and visit their websites. Often you can find information about who to talk to about a job, or even apply directly through an online portal.

- **Have an elevator pitch ready:** It helps to have a short, thirty-second introduction ready so you can quickly tell people who you are and what kind of job you're looking for. You could say something like, "I'm [your name]. I'm a high-school junior, and I'm hoping to find a summer job in banking. I've taken courses in business and economics, but I'm hoping to get some experience with a real company."
- **Play to your strengths:** Be sure to let potential employers know what you have to offer as an employee. Are you good at talking to people, in person or on the phone? Do you have great math skills?
- **Stay alert:** For someone who's underage, it's wise to be alert to how adults treat you. As an employee, you should be getting paid fairly, with deductions taken for taxes and Social Security. You should not be expected to be alone in the office, especially at night. If anyone talks or acts toward you in a way that makes you feel uncomfortable or threatened, don't stay silent. Go directly to your boss or their boss, your parents, a teacher, or another trusted adult and tell them what happened. You don't have to stay in a job where you don't feel safe.

Making Your Current Job Count

To become a financial manager, you need several years of experience in a related field. You may already be working in one of those jobs. Perhaps you're in a job closer to the entry level, for instance, bank teller. Or perhaps you feel you've gone as far as you want to in a mid-level role, for example, loan officer, accountant, securities sales agent, or financial analyst. You might be working in a different department in a company or other organization and be interested in making a lateral (sideways) move into the financial side.

Wherever you're starting, you can acquire the skills you need to make the jump. Be sure to read the next chapter to find out about gaining more education and certifications that can help you; and the final chapter, which talks about résumés and interviewing, as well as a section on talking to your boss about a promotion.

Networking means getting to know people who share your interests. *MangoStar_Studio/iStock/Getty Images*

Networking

What is networking? It can sound a little intimidating, but it's not all three-piece suits, cocktails, and elevator pitches. Networking is really just getting to know people who are interested in (or employed in) the same field that you're in or want to go into. Recent estimates say that between 70 percent and 85 percent of jobs are found through personal contacts, so it's important to get to know people and, when the time comes, let them know you're seeking a job in their field.

Another advantage of networking is the opportunity to meet mentors. A mentor is an experienced person who gives helpful advice to someone new to the field. Mentors can be teachers, supervisors, colleagues—anyone who knows more than you do, thinks highly enough of you to help you, and has valid advice to give.

So how do you start networking? By being active in the world and looking for opportunities to meet people who do what you'd like to do. For instance:

- **Clubs:** If your school has a business, economics, or math club, join it and be an active member. Invite people you'd like to learn from to come and speak to the club or give the club a tour of their offices.
- **Internships and jobs:** As you've already read, internships and summer or part-time jobs give you unique opportunities to learn from and get to know experienced professionals.
- **Professional organizations:** Some have student chapters or special events that students can attend. See the "Further Resources" section of this book to learn more, then check out their websites to see what's going on in your area.
- **Social media:** Some social media sites, for example, LinkedIn, let you connect with professional organizations as well as people in the field. *However*, just as with all social media, be wary of sharing personal information with people you don't know, especially if you are a minor.

INTERNAL VERSUS EXTERNAL NETWORKING

INTERNAL NETWORKING

Internal networking means reaching out to people you already know, for instance, at your school, your job, clubs, or local businesses. These people don't necessarily have to work in financial fields. They may have other advice or ideas that will help you on your journey. Be sure to give back, too. You don't want to be the one who is always asking for help but never giving any! Take care of these relationships. They are valuable in too many ways to list.

EXTERNAL NETWORKING

External networking means meeting new people at work, in clubs, in student chapters of professional associations, at conferences or workshops, or anywhere that you don't already spend a lot of time. If you discover someone you'd like to know or ask a question, seek them out and introduce yourself. Be polite and professional. Don't take up too much of his time, at least at first.

Summary

Now you know how to plan your plan! Everything you need to know is easily available to you. You just need to put out your hand and pick it up.

- First, be sure you know yourself.
- Next, figure out what you want out of your career.
- Know the different kinds of financial manager jobs out there.
- Understand what education and experience you need to achieve your goals.
- Ask for help when you need it.
- Get to know people by networking.
- Then plan your next move, and your next one!

Don't miss the "Further Resources" section in this book. You'll find plenty of additional sources to help you figure out your plan.

In the next chapter, "Pursuing the Education Path," we'll look at what kind of educational options are available and answer the most important question—how do you pay for it? Don't worry! It's easier than you might think.

LOLE NUÑEZ, FINANCIAL CENTER MANAGER

Lole Nuñez. *Courtesy of Lole Nuñez*

Lole Nuñez is the financial center manager for the University Federal Credit Union's (UFCU) Steck Financial Center in Austin, Texas. He holds a certified associate in project management (CAPM) certification. During his twenty-plus years in banking and credit unions, he has developed extensive expertise in branch operations, management, personnel hiring and training, and other leadership roles. *(Note: Credit unions use some different terminology than banks. Because credit unions are technically owned by their account holders, they say "members" where a regular bank would say "customers." A credit union financial center is similar to a bank branch.)*

What does a financial center manager do?

I oversee the operations of our center. We have standards or goals, operations, the way we have to do things. We have employees who need to be hired, developed—grown in their careers. I respond to a lot of escalations that aid the manager. Escalations are normally things like a member who needs something beyond the approval level of the personal banker, or an upset member who needs some help. Or they have a complex situation that our people need help with. I'll come in and help with that.

How did you decide to become a financial center manager?

I got into banking early. I'd just turned twenty, I was a young father, and I was looking for a good job. I had worked for one of these small loan companies, and I liked it, so I thought I'd like to get into banking. In 1991, it was hard to get into banking with little experience. My mother-in-law got me a job as a mailroom clerk at a bank. I got to meet a lot of people, and I got to know a lot of different departments. I got to know a couple of people who worked at the branches. I thought my skill set would work there, dealing directly with the customers. Then, when you look at that and think about how you want to grow, managing one of those centers is something where I thought I could do a good job. As a mailroom clerk, I knew a vice president who was over the branches at the bank. I went in one day in my mailroom shirt and asked if he had a second. Even though he was multiple levels above me (and above my boss), he agreed to mentor me. He would give me articles, things to read, just really supported my wish to learn more. He was really a big part of my wanting to move into this side of the house.

What is a typical day on your job?

We generally come in, and we like to have a morning huddle. That helps us get an idea of what we have going on for the day, what kind of appointments we have, if someone has training, lunch schedules, make sure we have all the people in the right places for that day. Sometimes you have to be flexible with the staff. A lot of times, the members who come in will dictate the way the day goes, depending on how busy we are. I have to respond to my boss and the things that she needs. I'm part of a lot of committees and projects that help our organization get better, more efficient at what we're doing. We're not small, but we are compared to really large banks. Throughout the day, a lot of coaching goes on, both unplanned and planned. A lot of e-mails and a lot of paperwork. I'm the kind of manager who likes to spend time in the lobby with the associates and welcoming members, so I do that, too.

What's the best part of being a financial center manager?

Absolutely, for me, it's the employee development piece. At this stage of my career, I've learned a lot! I look at my group here, and I have seventeen employees. They are younger, they're inexperienced, but I always think back to the guy who helped me. He gave me what I needed when I needed it. He wasn't there to teach me how to do a loan or an IRA. Everyone here is at different stages, so I have to know where they are and what coaching I can give them. If my people can leave me being a better person and banker than before they came, that's when I enjoy my job. I enjoy that journey.

What's the most challenging part of being a financial center manager?

Well, the older you are, you really have to work hard to get on the level of someone half your age, and it's not being as demanding of them as maybe my generation was on me. You have to work through a lot of generational differences. That can be a challenge. A twenty-one-year-old teller who lives at home doesn't have the same level of responsibility as someone else, so that's a challenge. The other thing is just managing the team dynamic. If I hire the wrong person, and it messes up the chemistry, that can set me back months. I'm very deliberate with that. I try to hire to fit with the dynamics of this team while still finding the most qualified person. But sometimes you don't know. I think I've had more good hires than bad, but sometimes you can tell within three months that it's not going to be a good fit. I've gotten a lot better at interviewing throughout my career. I spend a lot of time teaching others what I've learned related to hiring.

What's the most surprising thing about being a financial center manager?

I think, initially, it was always interesting how people came into this job who didn't have a long-term plan or view of what they wanted it to become. That was always a struggle to understand—you want to work here, you came here to work, but maybe it was just to have a job, to get a paycheck. Maybe it's because I really love working in financial services. I think it's strange when someone thinks of this as just a paycheck and not something they can grow in and create a nice career. Social purpose is so important to young people now. At a place like UFCU, that's something we can really help with. If you help someone, educate them, you can put them on a path for the next thirty years that will make them successful. Sometimes it seems like they look at banking as an older person's environment—"your dad's job." Turnover is amazing. It rarely happens with people older than thirty-five—they're there to stick it out a little bit longer.

How did (or didn't) your education prepare you to be a financial center manager?

If you're talking about someone who's a commercial or business banker, a certain kind of education helps them with analyzing financial statements and that kind of thing. As a financial center manager, the only education that helped me was deliberate learning that I did. I took a class called principles of banking—it didn't count toward college credit or anything, but I still have that book. I think I took that class in 1992. So much hasn't changed. I had to be very deliberate with a lot of that learning. Continuing education is paramount. I didn't have to get that project management certificate, but to move along in this industry, I needed to be more well-rounded. That was one area I wanted to learn more about.

Being a financial center manager is all about the people relationship—how you relate with your coworkers, employees, customers. You can't be much of an introvert and be successful at this. I was always someone you could have a conversation with, more outgoing. We had several introverts when I got here, and they struggled, because they weren't good at talking to people. I first got to be a financial center manager at the age of twenty-four because I was good with people. I was good with customers and coworkers. I was respectful of my superiors. I was a people person and a coach. I coached my kids' sports teams because that's what I enjoy doing. Being a coach and a financial center manager are kind of the same thing.

I didn't finish a college degree. I was going to school part-time, and then I became a manager and went from forty hours a week to fifty-five pretty quickly. That was sort of the end of that. A few years back, I thought about going to work for a bank that was closing branches and had a voluntary layoff. A career counselor said to me that my experience and intangibles are what's important for me. I don't know how easy it would be for me, if I were starting now, to become a financial center manager without a degree. It wasn't so much of an expectation then as it is now. It wasn't part of the job description. Now it's pretty much required unless you have a bunch of years of experience like me.

Is being a financial center manager what you expected?

Honestly, yes. Really, when I started out and I was learning, this is what I thought it would be. It's interesting—some financial center roles may change a little bit. Throughout my career, I've been a financial center manager *and* a mortgage officer, or a financial center manager *and* a business banker. I had both those roles at the same time. But for the most part, the core of what I do is what my mentor showed me many years ago.

What's next? Where do you see yourself going from here?

When you start looking at moving up the ladder beyond financial center manager, that's where not having the degree is a problem for me. It's kept me in this realm a bit. But the next step for me would be regional manager, unless I moved to a different business sector. For many financial center managers, they see regional manager as the next logical step. The next step up is to be your boss (that's what my boss is now). Unless you start going in different directions, for instance, business banking, investment services, or mortgage services, that's generally the next step. There are a lot fewer of those opportunities, and they come up with less frequency.

Where do you see the career of a financial center manager going from here?

You know, so much of that depends on the organization. Where I worked before, that bank has made the decision to move toward a consultative type of location, with coffee cafés in them. They have four or five in Boston, for instance. You go there, and you can't open an account, but they'll give you an iPad and show you how to do it yourself. Their goal is to advise you. I will say this—if I retire in sixteen years, branches will still be around, and they will still have managers. The hope is that they move to more of a consultative role, where you have mostly people who can provide financial advice. We have tellers here; they're very valuable, but they do a non-value-added transaction. If they make a deposit for you, you *could* have done it on your own through your ATM or mobile app. But if you come in and speak to someone, and they advise you on home loans, or making more money, or your credit—those are things that make a real impact on your financial future. There will be more people who can help you with those things, and the manager is the person who oversees that.

What is your advice for a young person considering this career?

I'll tell you the advice I give to the people I work with, as well as those who don't know anything about the industry.

For those I work with, I tell them you really need to be someone who cares about the future and the development of others. If you're concerned about just your-self and your paycheck, you won't be successful in the role. There are many jobs in banking or the credit union for people who want to make a lot of money. This isn't that job. It's been a great job for me. I've raised a family, just about paid off a house, have a 401K and all that. But to take a financial center manager role, you have to care about other people and their development and a little less about your own.

For those who are unfamiliar with the workings of a bank or a credit union, there are three ways to go. The way of leadership, the way of sales, and the way of operations. Someone in leadership needs to care about others more than him-self. Someone in sales is a little more about being an individual contributor, but he doesn't need to take responsibility for someone else's growth. Then you have op-erations—these are individuals who are taking care of things on the back end, the things that allow the salespeople and the leaders to do their jobs accurately so none of us go to jail. For leadership and sales, you need to be a people-person, who feels good about interacting with strangers every day. That's the thing that helped me become a financial center manager. I was good at interacting with strangers, extending my hand and greeting them, welcoming them to our bank. I did really well, because I was good at that.

Job fit is a big thing. There are roles for all kinds of people. One bank I used to work for likes to think of itself as a tech company that happens to be a bank. It has more analysts and project managers than branch staff. Many people have done great work for that organization or here at UFCU. There are analysts who work in the back; they're right for that job, and we're right for this one. When I was still working in the mailroom, and I was looking at jobs outside the mailroom, I'll admit there was a stigma on a mailroom guy—I think unfairly. I was applying for a back-office job, and a manager who knew me called me in and said, "Don't tell anybody, but you're better than this job. This job is back office, and you're going to move papers and click buttons. I've seen how you talk to people as you move through the halls. You need to be out front. You need to be the face of the bank." I was a little disappointed not to get that interview, but within four weeks I had a job as a teller. I know she was instrumental in getting me to that spot. But I think about what she said, and I think that holds true today.

Banking is an industry that makes you pay your dues. It's sometimes difficult to explain to people what that means. When you think about someone who finishes college and maybe has some student loan debt, that person doesn't really have any of the experience to get certain roles that pay a little more. You might come into a bank or credit union. You have a college degree (it almost doesn't matter what it's in), but your experience with the public is, say, working in a grocery store. So, I put them in a teller role, so they can learn that aspect of the business. That can be a surprise to people. It takes explaining and support for them to know that this is where you start, and you build your career from here. You don't start in the middle just because you have a degree. This industry isn't like that. But it can be a great long-term career.

3

Pursuing the Education Path

What Are Your Educational Options?

*I*f you aspire to be a financial manager, the first step is your education. Many financial managers majored in business, but as long as you learn about math, economics, accounting, and finance in the course of your education, you can major in anything you want to. It's certainly true that having a broad educational experience that includes liberal arts and humanities is an excellent basis for any career. (Think about all those "soft skills" you discovered you'll need back in chapter 2, as well as the "hard skills" that come with working with numbers.)

Education is your best path to success as a financial manager. *Prostock-Studio/iStock/Getty Images*

In most cases, a bachelor's degree is the essential starting point for a job as a financial manager. There are still cases where a person has started in an entry-level job without a college degree and worked their way up in to management, but nowadays, that's the exception, not the rule. You should assume that you'll need to begin with a bachelor's degree.

To move up into a management role, especially if you hope to go all the way to the top and become a chief financial officer (see the interview with La Vonda Williams in chapter 1), you should expect to earn a master's degree as well. In most cases, this would be a master of business administration (MBA) degree, although some other degrees could be relevant depending on the industry you work in.

Advanced certification, for example, as a certified public accountant (CPA), can also be helpful, depending on your organization's needs.

> The beautiful thing about learning is nobody can take it away from you.—B. B. King[1]

BACHELOR'S DEGREES

You can major in anything you want to—you can see by the interviews in this book that a wide range of majors can all lead to financial management careers. But if you already know that you want to become a financial manager, it could make sense to choose a major associated with that field.

Some possible majors to consider would be bachelor of science (BS) or bachelor of arts (BA) in the following:

- Accounting
- Banking and financial support services
- Business administration and management
- Business, management, and marketing
- Business/managerial economics
- Credit management
- E-commerce
- Economics
- Entrepreneurship
- Finance

- General business/commerce
- Human resources
- International finance
- Investments and securities
- Management information systems
- Management sciences and quantitative methods
- Marketing
- Math
- Not-for-profit management
- Organizational behavior
- Public finance
- Quantitative analysis/statistics
- Supply chain management/logistics

MASTER'S DEGREES

Earning a master's degree can make a big difference when you want to move up from an entry-level or mid-level career to a management position. If you decide to do a master's degree right after your bachelor's degree, you might want to look into colleges or universities that offer combined programs where you can earn an MBA or other master's degree in just one year.

If you're already working, adding a master's degree to your qualifications will make you even more promotable. It can be difficult to work in school around your work obligations. Some schools offer on-campus programs designed around the needs of working students. Many programs from reputable institutions are now available online as well. See the box entitled "Is Online Learning for You?"

Many different master's degrees are out there, and which one you pick depends on what you want from your degree. In general, choose an MBA if you want a program that offers a big-picture view of organizations, how they work, and how all the parts fit together. You might choose a more specialized degree, for instance, a master of science (MS) in finance, accounting, financial management, or another related area, if you want to specialize.

Some of the possible master's degrees to consider include the following:

- Master of business administration (MBA)
- MBA in accounting
- Master's in accounting (MAcc)
- Master of finance (MFin)
- Master of financial economics (MFE)
- Master of financial management (MFM)
- Master of quantitative finance (MQF)
- Master of science (MS) in accounting
- MS in accounting and fundamental analysis
- MS in finance
- MS in financial economics
- MS in management

PROFESSIONAL CERTIFICATIONS

Although financial managers are not required to hold any professional certifications, these additional credentials verify knowledge and competence. Some of the available certifications that may be helpful for a financial manager include:

- **Certified management accountant (CMA):** This certification signifies expertise in financial accounting and strategic management.
- **Certified public accountant (CPA):** CPAs are licensed by the state board of accountancy and must pass the American Institute of Certified Public Accountants (AICPA) exam.
- **Certified treasury professional (CTP):** The CTP designation is given by the Association for Financial Professionals (AFP) to finance professionals (especially treasurers and cash managers) who meet eligibility criteria and pass an exam.
- **Chartered financial analyst (CFA):** Conferred by the CFA Institute, CFA status goes to investment professionals who pass three exams and meet the education and experience requirements.

While knowledge is increasingly being viewed as a commodity or intellectual asset, there are some paradoxical characteristics of knowledge that are radically different from other valuable commodities. These knowledge characteristics include the following:

- Using knowledge does not consume it.
- Transferring knowledge does not result in losing it.
- Knowledge is abundant, but the ability to use it is scarce.
- Much of an organization's valuable knowledge walks out the door at the end of the day.

—Kimiz Dalkir[2]

Finding the College That's Right for You

There's so much information out there about how and why to choose a particular school for college. And there's so much to consider! How can you ever narrow it down and make the right decision?

The best way to be sure you can find the right place for you is to think about what matters to you and narrow your choices. Consider the different qualities in this section and make sure the schools you're considering offer what you're looking for.

On the other hand, don't narrow your list *too* far. You want to apply to several colleges or universities, not just one.

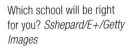
Which school will be right for you? *Sshepard/E+/Getty Images*

ACADEMIC ENVIRONMENT

The first thing you need to know is whether the school offers the major you want. What's involved in the degree program? What percentage of classes are taught by professors and what percentage are taught by adjunct instructors? Are adjunct instructors working professionals in the field? Does the school offer internships or cooperative education programs? Can you do a double major or a minor if you want to? Does it have a good reputation? (See the sidebar "Your School's Reputation.")

The place to find most of this information is on the university's website. Dig deep. Look at the name of the program, what courses are required, who the faculty members are (including their own research areas, which lets you know if they are active in their fields). Don't limit yourself to just the program's or department's page.

> Knowledge is indivisible. When people grow wise in one direction, they are sure to make it easier for themselves to grow wise in other directions as well. On the other hand, when they split up knowledge, concentrate on their own field, and scorn and ignore other fields, they grow less wise—even in their own field.—Isaac Asimov[3]

YOUR SCHOOL'S REPUTATION

One factor in choosing a college or certificate program is the school's reputation. This reputation is based on the quality of education previous students have had there. If you go to a school with a healthy reputation in your field, it gives potential employers a place to start when they are considering your credentials and qualifications.

Factors vary depending on which schools offer the program you want, so take these with a grain of salt. Some of the factors that affect reputation generally include:

- *Nonprofit or for-profit.* In general, schools that are nonprofit (or not-for-profit) organizations have better reputations than for-profit schools.
- *Accreditation.* Your program must be accredited by a regional accrediting body to be taken seriously in the professional world. It would be very rare to find an unaccredited college or university with a good reputation.

- *Acceptance rate.* Schools that accept a very high percentage of applicants can have lower reputations than those that accept a smaller percentage. That's because a high acceptance rate can mean there isn't much competition for those spaces, or that standards are not as high.
- *Alumni.* What have graduates of the program gone on to do? The college's or department's website can give you an idea of what its graduates are doing. The alumni office may host events where students can network with alumni.
- *History.* Schools that have been around a long time tend to be doing something right. They also tend to have good alumni networks, which can help you when you're looking for a job or a mentor.
- *Faculty.* Schools with a high percentage of permanent faculty versus adjunct faculty tend to have better reputations. Bear in mind that if you're going to a specialized program or certification program, this might be reversed—these programs are frequently taught by experts who are working in the field.
- *Departments.* A department at one school might have a better reputation than a similar department at a school that's more highly ranked overall. If your department is well known and respected, that could be more important than the reputation of the institution as a whole.

A lot of websites claim to have the "Top Ten Schools for Business" or "Best Twenty-Five Graduate Business Degrees." It's hard to tell which of those are truly accurate. So where to begin?

U.S. News & World Report is a great place to start to find a college or university with a great reputation. Go to https://www.usnews.com to find links to the highest-ranked schools for the undergraduate or graduate degree programs you're interested in.

SUPPORT SERVICES

Support services are such things as academic counseling, career counseling, health and wellness, residence services, the financial aid office, information technology support, commuter services, and services for students who have disabilities, or who have families, or who are lesbian, gay, bisexual, or transgender. Some schools also have religious support, for example, a chaplain. Before you choose a school, look through the website and be sure it provides the services you will need.

CLUBS/ACTIVITIES/SOCIAL LIFE

Most colleges have clubs and other social activities on campus, whether the student population is mostly residents or mostly commuters. Look for clubs related to the major you're interested in, as well as clubs and activities for your other interests. College campuses have all kinds of things going on all the time, for students and for the local community: concerts, comics, plays, open mic nights, game nights, art shows, and lots of other things. Don't miss out!

SPECIALIZED PROGRAMS

Does the school or program you're looking at have any programs that meet your specialized needs? For instance, some institutions have programs specifically for veterans. Some address learning disabilities or mental health issues. If you might benefit from a specialized program like these, be sure the school you attend can meet that need.

HOUSING OPTIONS

What kind of housing options do you want or need? Most four-year colleges and universities expect undergraduate students to live on campus. What are the dorms like? How many students will share a room? Graduate students might live on or off campus. Are there on-campus apartments? Will you need family student housing? Is there help with finding off-campus housing like apartments or rooms for rent? Be sure you have an affordable place to live!

TRANSPORTATION

If you live off campus, how will you get there? Is there a campus or city bus system? Is there a ride-share program? Could you ride a bicycle? Will you need to have access to a car? Is there an on-campus shuttle bus service that can get you around quickly if you're attending a large campus? Is there enough student parking?

STUDENT BODY

What's the makeup of the student body? What's the gender ratio? Is there enough diversity? Do most of the students live on campus, or are they commuters? Part-time or full-time students? Who will you meet there?

College is a great place to meet and get know other people who share your interests. It's also a great place to meet and get to know people who are very different from you. On a college campus, you'll encounter people from small towns and large cities, of all different ethnic backgrounds, different genders, different ages, studying or teaching many different topics. Be sure you take advantage of the opportunity to discover more kinds of people!

The Right Fit

As you look at the facts and figures, you also need to think about a less-quantifiable aspect of choosing a college or university: *fit*. What does that mean? It's hard to describe, but students know it when they feel it. It means finding the school that not only offers the program you want, but also the school that feels right. Many students have no idea what they're looking for in a school until they walk onto the campus for a visit. Suddenly, they'll say to themselves, "This is the one!"

While you're evaluating a particular institution's offerings with your conscious mind, your unconscious mind is also at work, gathering information about all kinds of things at lightning speed. When it tells your conscious mind what it's decided, we call that a "gut reaction." Pay attention to your gut reactions! There's good information in there.

IS ONLINE LEARNING FOR YOU?

During the COVID-19 pandemic, people learned a lot about learning online. From kindergartners through graduate students, classes moved onto Zoom and other interactive online formats. Even before that, many college and graduate students were looking to online programs as a way to save money on their degree programs and find a way to go to school without moving or giving up a much-needed job. Let's take a look at the pros and cons that have been discovered about online learning programs:

THE PROS

- You learn where you are. Especially important if you already have a job!
- You can learn at your own pace. Many online learning programs are set up so you can access what you need twenty-four hours a day/seven days a week.
- You can learn on your own schedule. Asynchronous classes let you work on course material and interact with your instructor when it's convenient for you.
- You have access to instructors. Some online programs have instructors from many different institutions, each bringing expertise from diverse locations.
- The interactive online learning environment can promote creative thinking and self-direction.
- It's easier to find programs (especially graduate programs) that work around your current career and other obligations.
- Online programs are usually significantly less expensive than on-campus programs; you also save on campus room and board, and many fees associated with campus-based programs.

THE CONS

- Online learning is harder than it looks. It can be difficult to stay motivated and do the work when learning remotely. To be successful as a remote learner, you have to motivate yourself and be purposeful about doing the work.
- There can be technology issues. To participate in an online learning program, you have to have a computer with the right specifications. There are lots of places where the tech can break down, cutting off participants from courses from time to time.
- You need internet access. You need reliable internet access to attend school online.
- You are missing out on the campus experience. In an online program, you won't have access to all the things to experience and people to meet that a campus provides.

- Building relationships online takes more effort and needs to be more intentional than in real life. The people you meet during your college years can end up being important to you, both personally and professionally, for the rest of your life. It's harder for your professors and classmates to get to know you as an individual.
- Subjects that require students to touch real things in a three-dimensional environment often don't work well for online learning.

Online instruction can only be as good as the instructor is at teaching this way. Instructors need to know how to create classroom rapport and support learning in a nontraditional environment.

What Will It Cost You?

Costs can be quite different, depending on the degree program you choose. And a lot of other factors affect the cost of your undergraduate or graduate education. Are you going straight to a four-year school, or could you do your first two years at a community college and transfer to finish your bachelor's degree? Public or private? How much financial aid are you eligible for in terms of scholarships or grants? How much will you be expected to borrow in student loans?

> If a man empties his purse into his head no one can take it away from him. An investment in knowledge always pays the best interest.—Benjamin Franklin (attributed)[4]

Table 3.1 is taken from information available on the College Board website[5] (www.collegeboard.org) and represents the estimated costs for undergraduate students during the 2020–2021 academic year.

Table 3.1.   Estimated Costs for Full-Time Undergraduate Budgets, 2020–2021.

	Tuition and Fees	Room and Board	Books and Supplies	Transportation	Other Expenses	Total
Private Nonprofit Four-Year On-Campus	$37,650	$13,120	$1,240	$1,060	$1,810	$54,880
Public Four-Year Out-of-State On-Campus	$27,020	$11,620	$1,240	$1,230	$2,170	$43,280
Public Four-Year In-State On-Campus	$10,560	$11,620	$1,240	$1,230	$2,170	$26,820
Public Two-Year In-District Commuter	$3,770	$9,080	$1,460	$1,840	$2,400	$18,550

NOTES: Expense categories are based on institutional budgets for students as reported in the College Board's Annual Survey of Colleges. Figures for tuition and fees and room and board mirror those reported in Table 1. Books and supplies may include the cost of a personal computer used for study. Other expense categories are the average amounts allotted in determining the total cost of attendance and do not necessarily reflect actual student expenditures.

That's a lot of money! *However,* these are averages. You'll need to look closely at the costs of the schools you're considering—they could be quite different from these. In general, tuition and other costs for college tend to go up about 3 percent every year, so take that into consideration when planning for the year that you'll be going to school.

But don't worry! There are all kinds of ways to bring down those costs!

Paying for college is about more than just saving your pennies. *Marchmeena29/iStock/Getty Images*

FINANCIAL AID

It can really pay off to put some time and effort into discovering what financial aid you qualify for. Reach out to the financial aid office at the school you want to attend. They can tell you a lot about what you may be able to work out.

Financial aid can come from many sources. The kind of awards you're eligible for depend on a lot of things, including the following:

- Academic performance in high school
- Financial need
- Program/field
- Type of college

NOT ALL FINANCIAL AID IS CREATED EQUAL

Educational institutions tend to define financial aid as any scholarship, grant, loan, or paid employment that assists students to pay their college expenses. Notice that "financial aid" covers both *money you have to pay back* and *money you don't have to pay back*. That's a big difference!

DO NOT HAVE TO BE REPAID

- Scholarships
- Grants
- Work-study

HAVE TO BE REPAID *WITH INTEREST*

- Federal government loans
- Private loans
- Institutional loans

SCHOLARSHIPS

Scholarships are financial awards that are usually offered on the basis of academic merit, membership in a particular organization, or for people going into a particular field. Scholarships can also be available to students who meet certain criteria (e.g., athletes, students from a particular high school) or who are underrepresented in a particular field or major. Some scholarships go toward tuition; others are for such things as textbooks and school supplies.

> College may seem expensive. But the truth is that most students pay less than their college's sticker price, or published price, thanks to financial aid. So instead of looking at the published price, concentrate on your net price—the real price you'll pay for a college. . . . Your net price is a college's sticker price for tuition and fees minus the grants, scholarships, and education tax benefits you receive. The net price you pay for a particular college is specific to you because it's based on your personal circumstances and the college's financial aid policies.—BigFuture™[6]

Scholarships usually pay part (not all) of tuition—it is rare to receive a full-tuition scholarship, but it does happen. Scholarships do not have to be paid back. Scholarships can be local, regional, statewide, or national in scope.

There are also scholarships specifically for community college students, including those who want to transfer to a bachelor's degree program later on or those who are studying a particular subject. Some are offered by professional associations, some by nonprofit organizations, and some by the community colleges themselves.

GRANTS

Grants are similar to scholarships. Most tuition grants are awarded based on financial need, but some are restricted to students in particular sports, academic fields, demographic groups, or with special talents. Grants do not have to be paid back.

Some grants come through federal or state agencies, for example, the Pell Grant, SMART Grants, and Federal Supplemental Education Opportunity Grant (FSEOG). You'll need to fill out the FAFSA form (see the section on "Loans"). Learn more about those at studentaid.ed.gov/types /grants-scholarships.

Grants can also come from private organizations or from the college itself. For instance, some private colleges or universities have enough financial resources that they can "meet 100 percent of proven financial need." That doesn't mean a free ride, but it usually means some grant money to cover the gap between what the financial aid office believes you can afford and the amount that scholarships and federal loans cover (more on federal loans below).

WORK-STUDY

The federal work-study program provides money for undergraduate and graduate students to earn money through part-time jobs. Work-study is a need-based program, so you'll need to find out if you are eligible for it. Some students are not eligible at first but become eligible later in their college career. Most jobs are on campus, some relate to your field, but others—for instance, working in the library—could be more general.

Some colleges and universities don't participate in the work-study program, so check with the financial aid office to see if it's available and if you're eligible for it. It's good to apply early to have a better chance of getting the job you want most.

Because work-study is earned money (you do a job and get paid for it), this money does not need to be paid back. To learn more, check out studentaid.ed.gov/sa/types/work-study.

LOANS

A gap almost always exists between tuition and the amount of money you receive from a school in scholarships and grants. That gap is filled by student loans. Student loans have to be repaid. Interest varies depending on the type of loan. Be sure you understand how much interest you will be charged, when the interest starts to accumulate, and when you must start paying back the loan. Usually, repayment starts when you graduate or after a six-month grace period.

Federal Loans

Federal student loans are issued by the U.S. government. They have lower interest rates and better repayment terms than other loans. You don't need anyone to cosign for your debt. If the loan is *subsidized*, the federal government pays the interest until you graduate. If it's *unsubsidized*, interest starts to accrue as soon as you accept the loan. That can amount to a very big difference in how much you pay for your education by the time the loan is paid off.

The most common federal student loan is the low-interest Federal Stafford Loan, which is available to both undergraduate and graduate students. Depending on household income, a student's Stafford loan might be subsidized or unsubsidized. *(Note: the federal Perkins loan is no longer available.)*

Most schools will require you to fill out the FAFSA when you apply for financial aid. FAFSA stands for Free Application for Federal Student Aid. Note that it doesn't say "free student aid." It says "free application." That means it does not cost anything to apply for federal student aid. You may get "offers" to submit the FAFSA for you for a fee—this is a scam. Don't do it.

Private Loans

Chances are, federal student loans will not completely fill the gap between your tuition bill and any scholarships or grants you receive. Private student loans are issued by a bank or other financial institution. Rates of interest are generally higher than for federal loans, so be careful not to borrow more than you need. Eligibility criteria for private loans are based on your credit (and your cosigner's credit) history.

Don't just take the first loan you find. Do some research; compare interest rates and terms. Is the interest variable or fixed? Does the variable interest have a cap? Is the company reputable? What are the repayment requirements?

Institutional Loans

Many educational institutions make their own loans, using funds provided by such donors as alumni, corporations, and foundations, as well as from repayments made by prior college loan borrowers. Every college will have its own rules, terms, eligibility, and rates. Interest may be lower than private student loans, and the deferment option may be better as well.

Learn more about all kinds of financial aid through the College Board website at bigfuture.collegeboard.org/pay-for-college.

FINANCIAL AID TIPS

- Some colleges/universities offer tuition discounts to encourage students to attend—so tuition costs can be lower than they look at first.
- Apply for financial aid during your senior year of high school. The sooner you apply, the better your chances. Check out fafsa.gov to see how to get started.
- Compare offers from different schools—one school may be able to match or improve on another school's financial aid offer.
- Keep up your grades—a good GPA helps a lot when it comes to merit scholarships and grants.
- You have to reapply for financial aid every year, so you'll be filling out that FAFSA form again!
- Look for ways that loans might be deferred or forgiven—service commitment programs are a way to use service to pay back loans.

While You're in College

Once you're enrolled in an undergraduate degree program, of course, you'll take all the classes that your major requires. And you'll take advantage of everything college has to offer. College will be time consuming and a lot of hard work, as it should be. But there's more to your college experience than that!

One of the great advantages of college is that it's so much more than just training for a particular career. It's your opportunity to become a broader, deeper person, to understand the world in fuller, more complete, and more interesting ways. Use your electives to take courses far outside your major. Join clubs, intramural teams, singing groups—whatever catches your interest. Take a foreign language. The broader your world view is, the more interesting you are as a person—and the more appealing you are to employers in the future!

In a graduate program, you'll dig deeper into your degree field. You'll learn more about it, from the big picture to the details. You'll also meet people—colleagues and professors—who share your interests. You'll form friendships and business relationships that will be very important to you going forward, among a broader range of people than you meet at your job every day.

Class participation helps you learn! *FatCamera/E+/Getty Images*

It has always seemed strange to me that in our endless discussions about education so little stress is laid on the pleasure of becoming an educated person, the enormous interest it adds to life. To be able to be caught up into the world of thought—that is to be educated.—Edith Hamilton[7]

WORKING WHILE YOU LEARN

You'll learn a lot about business and finance while you're working on your degree. But that doesn't always convey what it's like to do the work in real life. If you have the opportunity, consider trying some of these ways to learn and work at the same time.

Internships

Internships are another way to gain work experience while you're in school. Internships are offered by employers and usually last one semester or one summer. You might work part-time or full-time, but you're usually paid in experience and college credit rather than money. Some fields have paid internships, but they aren't common. Your campus career office or department chair are good places to start to learn about internships for college students. Be sure to check back to chapter 2 for advice on internships.

Cooperative Education Programs

Cooperative education (co-op) programs are a structured way to alternate classroom instruction with on-the-job experience. All kinds of careers have co-op programs. They are run by the educational institution in partnership with several employers. Students usually alternate semesters in school with semesters at work. Be sure the college you attend is truly committed to its co-op program. Some are deeply dedicated to the idea of co-ops as integral to education, but others treat it more like an add-on program.

A co-op program is different from an internship. Students in co-op jobs typically work forty hours a week during their work semesters and are paid a regular salary. Participating in a co-op program means it will take longer to graduate, but you come out of school with a lot of legitimate work experience. The company you co-op with is not obliged to hire you at the end of the program. But it can still be an excellent source of good references for you in your job search.

Part-Time Job

It can be hard to hold down a full-time job while enrolled full-time in a degree program (although many people manage to do this, especially if they're professionals working toward an advanced degree). Finding a part-time job in a financial institution, an insurance company, or almost any kind of business can help you build experience for your résumé while learning about how businesses work in real life.

Start by dropping into your campus Career Office to see if they can provide you with any job leads. And talk to your instructors and other people you meet to let them know you're looking—you never know who may know something that will help!

Financial Management for Financial Managers

There's something else you can learn, while you're in college or even before! When you're young and first starting out in life, all the different expenses you face can really take you by surprise. But if you want to be a financial manager, it's important to be able to manage your own finances.

Learning to manage your own finances and plan for the future is essential for up-and-coming financial managers. *Takasuu/iStock/Getty Images*

NerdWallet[8] has some good advice for when you're starting to manage your own money. Here's the abbreviated version:

- **Create a simple budget:** Try the 50/30/20 approach. That's 50 percent on needs (rent, groceries, utilities, and loan payments), 30 percent on splurges (trips, concerts, takeout), and 20 percent on savings and extra debt payments.
- **Make a money priorities list:** Emergency fund (at least $500 cash); retirement; pay off high-interest debt first; then grow your emergency fund to three to six months' worth of expenses.

- **Plan for retirement:** Fund your retirement plan to the fullest extent possible. If your employer matches 401(k) contributions, that's part of your compensation package—you earned it. Don't miss out. If you don't have a 401(k) or 403(b) plan, start an IRA and plan to contribute 15 to 20 percent of your income every month. "Every $1,000 invested at age 22 becomes nearly $20,000 when you are 72, assuming a 6% rate of return."[9]
- **Understand your student loan debt:** Private, public, or a combination? How much do you owe? At what interest rate? What happens if you pay early? Can you consolidate, and would that be a good idea for you?
- **Learn about investing:** Start with a reliable source of information, for example, the Investor Protection Trust (IPT) website (investorprotec tion.org). Watch out for hype and pressure to invest in something too soon or too fast.
- **Be careful with credit:** Know your credit score and what it means. Use a credit card to establish credit and build a good score, but pay it off in full every month. Don't charge more than you could pay cash for. It's easy to get in over your head with credit cards. Be disciplined.

It's never too early to start learning how to manage your own finances!

Summary

In this chapter, you've taken a look at how to approach your college and/or graduate school education. You've considered different majors and learned about what to look for in an on-campus experience when you're choosing a school. You've learned about financial aid options and ways to think about them. And you've learned a bit about the difference between studying in a classroom versus studying online. It's a lot to take in and a lot to consider! But it's well worth the effort to find the educational experience that's right for you and works with your lifestyle and your plans.

In the final chapter, we're going to look at how you begin finding and applying for jobs that will lead to a career as a financial manager and the skills you'll need to succeed. We'll take a look at how to put together a résumé and write a cover letter, interview skills, and even what to wear. But, first, see what Jillian White has to say about her career as a credit manager for a bank.

It won't be long until you graduate and prepare to enter the working world! *Sam Edwards/iStock/Getty Images*

JILLIAN WHITE, CREDIT MANAGER

Jillian White. *Courtesy of Jillian White*

Jill White is a credit manager at a regional bank in New England. She holds a BS in business administration from Plymouth State University and an MS in accounting from Southern New Hampshire University. Her background is in commercial credit analysis and underwriting, with special concentration in the areas of commercial real estate, small business, middle market, municipal, not-for-profit, and C&I (commercial and industrial). She is certified by the Center for Financial Training as a business credit analyst and as a business credit and tax return analyst. She also serves as a volunteer adjudicator for the Annual Future Business Leaders of America Conference.

What does a credit manager do?

I manage a team of credit analysts and their workflow. As the credit manager, I'm tasked with protecting the bank's loan portfolio, making sure we're not taking on too much risk or that riskier loans are structured to protect the bank. We handle loan underwriting, which is the process of accumulating all the financial information about a potential loan or investment to a business and evaluating it for approval. The analysts take the data and use this information to essentially tell the story of the business. The company provides us with its financial data, for instance, annual reports, tax returns, and industry-specific numbers (e.g., the occupancy rate for a hotel). Then the analysts evaluate all the data to see what kind of risk it might pose and how it relates to the request for financing. Then they take all these numbers and put them into a presentation, which is usually brought into committee to be voted on or can be approved by certain individuals within the bank. Analysis is the nitty-gritty—the core of what we do. Being a good analyst means you're able to interpret the numbers and put them into a format where someone who doesn't have a background in that specific business could easily pick up the presentation and say, "I understand what's going on."

How did you decide to become a credit manager?

I started as a credit analyst almost straight out of college. I had never thought of this as a career path for me, because growing up I didn't know this kind of role existed within a bank. I'd always been interested in working in a bank. While working a temporary job, I was looking for opportunities in banking and found my first credit analyst position. I fell in love with it—that it's basically taking the financial statements that a business provides to the bank, and then making sense of them and ultimately making a recommendation about whether investing in the business is a palatable risk to the bank. I started as an entry-level credit analyst and worked my way up through senior level. I also explored portfolio management, which is a blend between a lender and a credit analyst, because you're dealing more directly with customers. After a couple of years as portfolio manager, I had the opportunity to become a credit manager, which was really my goal all along.

What is a typical day on your job?

I start my day checking in with all the members of my team, individually or as a group, making sure everyone has work to do and is on pace and able to meet their deadlines. The rest of my day varies depending on the day. I could be meeting with individual members of the team to discuss new deals assigned to them, critique their work, or provide training. I could be meeting with lenders to discuss deals they want to bring into the department. I also help my own manager with reports, so I might be doing internal reporting or projects. Training is a big part of what I do, either one-on-one or in groups, so I take time to develop training programs for not only my own team, but also other bank employees. I act as backup for my underwriting team if they need assistance communicating with lenders or management as well. It's a full day!

What's the best part of being a credit manager?

When I feel like I've taught somebody something new, and they've understood and accomplished it. To take them from zero to being a full-fledged analyst—that to me is the best. It's so satisfying, and it makes me so proud! As much as being an analyst is an "individual sport," you're also part of a team. You're responsible for your own performance, but you also have the support of your team, cheering you on and helping you.

What's the most challenging part of being a credit manager?

For me personally, some of the aspects of people management. You want to be the approachable manager and not the person who's up on a throne. You want to be someone people can come to, but you don't want to be a pushover. Sometimes you have to do the things that aren't fun. You might have to discipline an employee or address poor performance, and sometimes you have to let people go. That's hard, because you invest a lot as a manager in your team, emotionally and professionally. That part of being a manager doesn't come easily to a lot of people.

What's the most surprising thing about being a credit manager?

I was surprised at how full my day would get! Not that I thought I'd be sitting around, doing nothing and waiting for people to come to me, but I was very surprised at how my attention gets divided. As the credit manager, you're expected to know where your team is with each deal they're working on at all times, which really tests your multitasking ability. If you haven't already learned how to prioritize and manage your time, you'll learn that pretty quickly.

How did (or didn't) your education prepare you to be a credit manager?

I think my education prepared me from a technical standpoint. High school and college honed my writing, math, and basic accounting knowledge. My master's degree prepared me for the accounting questions. But as far as people management—that is something I didn't get from my degree. That's something I've been learning and picking up as I go. I always think, "What kind of boss would I want to work for?" Education tries to give you a taste of what it means to be a manager or a leader when you have group projects. Someone always takes the leader role: they delegate, accumulate all the work, and put it all together at the end. That's one way that school does teach you about management. So, if you're interested in management, take on that leadership role and see if you like it.

Is being a credit manager what you expected?

Yes! I think it is. I worked really closely with the credit manager at one of my previous banks. He was a great mentor, and I really looked up to him. It is what I expected it to be—and more. I have a little more of an investment in the people who are working for me. I feel a little more connected than if I were just another member on the team.

What's next? Where do you see yourself going from here?

Ultimately, my career goal is to become a senior credit officer, whether at my current bank or somewhere else. I see myself going toward credit risk or overall risk management within the bank.

Where do you see the career of a credit manager going from here?

I think it's a pretty steady career. The demand for credit analysts is definitely there. The size of the department and the amount of work will dictate whether a bank requires a credit manager. In terms of advancement, if people are looking to move up from credit manager, they're usually on the track of becoming a senior credit officer. Or they might branch off into the risk management that occurs in the "back of the house" of bank operations—like managing the allowance for losses and troubled loans.

What is your advice for a young person considering this career?

This is a great career for someone who always likes to learn something new. See if you can start with an internship or at the junior credit analyst level. That's a good stepping-stone if you want to try it on for size. You learn a lot. A lot is thrown at you at once, but if you're a fast learner and have an aptitude for writing, math, and accounting, you could find it's the right fit for you. Promotion along the track from junior analyst to credit analyst to senior analyst may be rapid or it may be slow, depending on your skill and your employer. The underlying principles of accounting is what drives analysis, so if you have a strong grasp of accounting principles and good communication skills but maybe don't want to be an accountant, credit analysis could be a great option for you. It's an area that doesn't get boring because it involves so many different kinds of businesses and types of analysis. You could be looking at a country club one day, and the next day a roller rink, and the next day a marina, and the next day a hotel. It's so varied, depending on where you live and what businesses are predominant in that area. There are also banks that specialize in certain types of lending, for instance, manufacturing, commercial real estate, or municipal lending. There's always something new to learn, no matter how long you've worked in underwriting.

Getting the Job—Résumés and Interviewing

Stepping In or Stepping Up?

*W*hen you first graduate from college, you'll probably be hired for an entry-level or perhaps a mid-level job rather than be hired directly as a financial manager. If you've been working in a related field for several years, you may be looking for a promotion or a financial manager job with a different employer.

Get ready to join the team! *Chris Ryan/iStock/Getty Images*

In either case, having a résumé and cover letter that show you at your best will help you achieve your goals. Good interviewing skills let the other person know that you approach your career in a positive and professional way. To continue that professional impression, you need to act and dress the part once you have the job.

But before you can do any of that, you first have to find a job to apply for!

Where to Find Financial Manager Jobs

Where do you begin your job search? How do you find companies that are hiring? Don't worry—jobs for financial managers or leading to that career are available in communities from small to large, in small and mid-sized businesses and large corporations, in the for-profit sector and in nonprofit institutions from universities to hospitals and more.

Just as you did in chapter 2, it helps to make a list of what you're looking for in a job and potential resources that can help you find the right job.

YOUR COLLEGE OR UNIVERSITY CAREER CENTER

While you're still in school, working on your bachelor's or master's degree, drop by the campus Career Center. This office exists to help you get a job. They maintain listings for all different kinds of jobs, and they can give you great advice about where and how to find jobs to apply for. They'll also review your résumé and give you tips to make it better.

Even after you graduate, the Career Center can still help. Most colleges and universities continue to provide help to their alumni through the campus Career Center.

Many schools also host events or provide lists of their alumni who are already working in certain fields and who are willing to help new graduates find a position. These can be important networking opportunities!

Speaking of networking . . .

NETWORKING

Some say the best way to find a job is through networking. Your personal and professional contacts may know about an upcoming job that hasn't even been advertised yet. Sometimes, an employer may even create a position for someone they want to hire. Keep in touch with the people you know in the field, at every level, and let them know that you're available.

Still wondering about how to network? Flip back to chapter 2 and check out the "Networking" section.

PROFESSIONAL ORGANIZATIONS

One of the services that most professional organizations provide is a list of open positions. Employers post jobs here because organization members are often the most qualified and experienced. The "Further Resources" section in this book lists numerous professional organizations and associations. Be sure to ask your instructors and employed friends about which associations you should look into. You can also search online to find out which organizations to join and where the best source of job information is likely to be.

CHECK THE LISTINGS

Most employers will advertise open positions online on employment sites. Other sites aggregate this information and pull it all together. Here are just a few of the options:

- **LinkedIn:** Create a LinkedIn page for yourself and fill it with all of your qualifications and experience. Then click on Jobs on the menu at the top of the page and fill in the keywords and location in the boxes that appear. LinkedIn is a useful site because you can do more than just upload your résumé—you can also maintain professional connections with other people and businesses.
- **Résumé sites:** You can upload your résumé on many sites on the internet, and it doesn't cost you anything to do so.

Don't use one that charges you! Some of the most recognized include the following:

- CareerBuilder
- Glassdoor
- Indeed
- Monster
- TheMuse
- ZipRecruiter

Note: This alphabetical list does not constitute an endorsement of any particular site.

- **Direct search:** Even if you don't want to list your résumé on any of these sites, when you enter the job-hunting terms into your favorite search engine, job listings from these sites will come up.
- **Company websites:** Most larger employers (and even some small ones) have a page on their website labeled "Careers" or "Work with Us" or "Employment" that has information about current job openings and how to apply for them. Some will accept your résumé even if they don't have any listed positions at the moment.

Writing Your Résumé

WHAT IS A RÉSUMÉ?

A résumé is just a brief, written list of what you've done and where you learned to do it. It may also include any honors you've earned or special things you've done or been a part of. A printed résumé should usually be one to two pages long.

You submit your résumé (along with a cover letter) whenever you apply for a job. You may also want to upload your résumé to a few of the many résumé sites available on the internet and use it as the basis for a page on LinkedIn.

TYPES OF RÉSUMÉS

There are three basic formats for a résumé.

Your résumé sums up who you are, what you know, and what you've done. *Jakkapant turasen/ iStock/Getty Images*

Reverse Chronological Résumé

The reverse chronological résumé is the most traditional format. It's written with the most current information first, going backwards to the oldest information last. This type of résumé works for everyone, whether you're a student or already working. It's the easiest to use when you want to fill in an online or paper application form. The usual layout is pretty simple.

- Name and contact information at the top
- Education, starting with most recent first (if you have a college degree, you don't need to include your high school). When you're at the beginning of your career, list education first. When you're more experienced, move the education section after the experience section.
- Qualifications like specialized certifications
- Professional experience with job title, dates of employment (month or year is fine), and a short, bulleted list of your duties and accomplishments
- Military service (if any)
- Awards and honors (if any)
- Volunteer experience (if relevant)

Functional Résumé

A functional résumé is designed to highlight your skills and qualifications rather than your work history. Also called a skills résumé, the functional résumé shows that you're a strong candidate for a job, plays down periods of time when you weren't employed or were working in an unrelated field. A functional résumé helps employers focus on specific skills needed for the job they're hiring for. It's all about making sure the employer can focus on what's relevant to the job in question.

For a functional résumé, break up your information into several categories that describe your skills. The categories should be in the order of most importance to the *potential employer*. Within each category, you'll include a bulleted list of examples. These should also be in order of importance, rather than by date. Include a synopsis of your work experience. The usual layout for a functional résumé is as follows:

- Name and contact information at the top
- Summary of your skills and abilities
- Qualifications like certification and licensing
- Awards and honors (if any)
- Relevant skill blocks in order of importance, for example, technical skills, business skills, people skills
- Professional experience with job title, dates of employment (month or year is fine). Include short, bulleted items about your duties and accomplishments if the jobs are different from each other in a significant way (otherwise, you've already covered this in the skill blocks).
- Education, starting with most recent first (if you've been to college, you don't need to list your high school)
- Volunteer experience (if relevant)

Combined Résumé

A combined résumé is the best of both worlds. It combines aspects of both the reverse chronological résumé and the functional résumé. A combined résumé is best for someone with job experience, so that you have something to summarize. It highlights your skills while still showing your impressive employment history.

Like a functional résumé, the combined résumé begins with a professional summary of your skills, abilities, and achievements that are specifically relevant to the job opening. Then your education and experience follow in reverse chronological order.

Use a combined résumé in the following instances:

- You want to focus on your knowledge and accomplishments.
- You want to highlight your relevant experience.
- You're applying for a job that requires technical skills and expertise.
- You want to move into a new field.
- You want to demonstrate mastery in your field.

The usual layout for a combined résumé is pretty simple.

- Name and contact information at the top
- Summary of your skills and abilities
- Qualifications like certification and licensing
- Professional experience with job title, dates of employment (month or year is fine). Include short, bulleted items about your duties and accomplishments if the jobs are different from each other in a significant way (otherwise you've already covered this in the skill blocks).
- Awards and honors (if any)
- Education, in reverse chronological order
- Volunteer experience (if relevant)

Writing Your Cover Letter

Your cover letter is the short, personalized letter that you send with your résumé to introduce yourself to a potential employer. A well-written cover letter is a way to show a little of your personality, to highlight where and how your background makes a good fit for the position you want, and to indicate your interest in working for that employer.

You should always try to send your letter (with your résumé) to the person who is responsible for making the hiring decision. Only if you absolutely cannot find out who that person is should you send it to the human resources office.

Your letter should be in business letter format. Be sure your name and contact information are at the top of the letter, either centered or on the right.

- Address the reader by name—avoid such generic greetings as "Dear Manager" or "Dear Director." Use Ms. or Mr. with the last name. (Do not use Miss or Mrs. unless you have been specifically instructed to do so.)
- Identify the specific position you are interested in and where you heard about it (some companies like to track how applicants heard about the position so they know which recruiting methods are working best). Mention that your résumé is included or attached.
- If you heard about the opening from a specific person, mention that person by name.
- Highlight your most relevant qualifications: skills that match the ones in the job description and/or skills that could transfer to those in the job description. Focus on your strengths and on what you could bring to the position. Think about this from the employer's point of view—what about your background will benefit them?
- Avoid negative language—phrase everything in a positive way. In particular, avoid complaining about a previous employer or customer.
- Your conclusion should include a confident call to action, for example, requesting an interview. Don't ask directly for the job, just an interview at this point. Include your phone number here, as well as with your contact information at the top.
- Closing: Sincerely. (That's it. Don't use any other word.)
- Add a few lines of space for your signature, then type your name.
- Sign the letter by hand

If you are applying for the position via e-mail, you can either copy and paste it into the body of your e-mail or save the letter as a pdf and attach it to the e-mail along with your résumé.

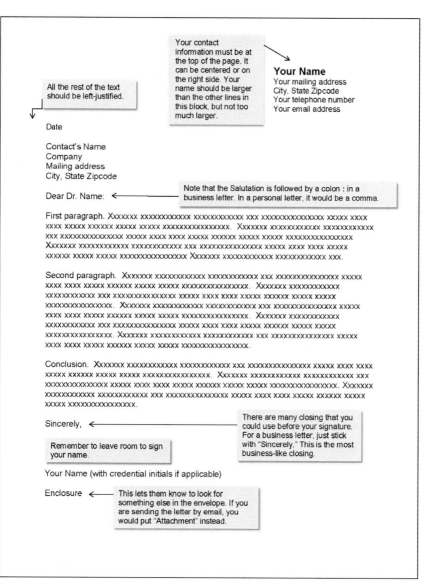

Sample cover letter.

GETTING TO YES

A lot of work leads to a career in financial management, and you will probably find a job sooner than you think. But you have no guarantee that you will be offered *the job of your dreams* when you first start looking. Here are some tips that will improve your chances of "getting to yes."

- Do your research. Find out about the company that you want to apply to.
- Talk to people—especially people you know already or friends of friends.
- Ask about what the potential employer is like to work for.
- Ask about what they value in their employees.
- Ask about benefits and the general pros and cons of working there.
- If you're qualified for a specific job opening, apply for it!
- If there isn't a specific job opening, write to the head of the company or department you're interested in, mention your contacts, and ask if they would have a conversation with you about potential openings.
- Be flexible—you might find a good job in a different location than you wanted or doing something slightly different than you originally planned.
- Put your best self forward—everyone you meet is a potential contact for a job (or maybe just a new friend).
- If you get an interview, don't forget that all-important thank-you note! It's one of the most important things you can do to make a good impression. Send the note *that day*, as soon after the interview as possible.
- Don't put all your eggs in one basket—apply for lots of jobs at the same time.

DEALING WITH NO

A wise person once said, "If they didn't hire you, you probably would not have been happy working there anyway." Both employers and employees need to find the right fit. If they didn't think you were the right fit, you most likely wouldn't have thought so after a while either. Here are some tips to weather the noes while you're waiting for the yeses.

- Apply for lots of jobs at the same time, so no one job will be too important to you.

- It doesn't feel great to be turned down for a job, but try not to take it personally.
- Don't burn your bridges! Don't retaliate with an angry letter or e-mail, or troll the company all over social media. Another opportunity may come up there or with someone they know.
- Keep improving your résumé and your cover letter.
- Keep putting your best self forward—even if you're feeling discouraged, pick up your head and go through your day shining with confidence.
- Work your contacts—talk to other people you know. They may know an employer who would be a great match for you.
- Take advice—if someone (especially at or following an interview) tells you that you need to improve something, *improve it*. This may be an additional credential, or something about your interpersonal skills, or your spelling, or your breath, or whatever. If someone tells you something about yourself that you don't like to hear but suspect may be right, don't get mad. Get better.
- Keep doing your research, so if one employer turns you down, you have three more to apply to that day.
- Keep telling yourself that employment is just around the corner. Then make it true!

The Interview

An interview is a business meeting where a prospective employer is checking you out. Don't forget that you are also checking them out. You are both there to see if it would be a good fit for you to work together. No matter how much you want the job, remember that you are not there to beg for charity—you are there to offer your services in your professional role.

It's important to make a good impression when you're applying for a job at any level. Be your best self, be confident, be polite.

Good interviewing skills will make you a top candidate for any job. *SeventyFour/iStock/Getty Images*

INTERVIEWING TIPS

- **Be on time:** Don't be late, *ever*. Try to arrive ten to fifteen minutes early so you have time to go into the restroom and check yourself in the mirror before you go into the interview. And don't be too early—that's just awkward.
- **Dress appropriately:** See the section below on how to dress.
- **Bring your résumé:** Yes, they already have it. Bring extra copies just in case. It's helpful and shows that you're the kind of person who is prepared.
- **Smile:** Let them know that you will be a pleasant person to work with.
- **Shake hands well (or don't):** A firm handshake marks you as a person to be taken seriously. It's traditional to shake hands as you enter the meeting and again before you leave. After the COVID-19 pandemic, not everyone is comfortable shaking hands. Take the lead from the person you're meeting.

- **Ask for a business card:** You may meet with just one person, with a committee, or with several people individually. At the end of the meeting, ask for a business card from each person so that you have good contact information for thank-you notes (see below).
- **Have good posture:** Sit up straight, make reasonable eye contact (not staring, not avoiding), keep your shoulders back. Make it look normal, though—like you always sit or stand that way. Good posture conveys energy and enthusiasm for the job. Slouching or avoiding eye contact makes you look bored.
- **Be prepared:** Learn about the company ahead of time so that you sound knowledgeable during the interview. Read their website, talk to people.
- **Be ready to answer questions:** At a job interview, you can expect to be asked some standard questions ("Where do you see yourself in five years?") and more specific questions that let you show you know your stuff.
- **Don't be afraid to ask questions:** Some people don't like to ask questions in an interview because they think it makes them look ignorant. Actually, *not* asking questions makes them look uninterested. Have some questions prepared—both basic and more in depth, because the basic ones might be answered before you have a chance to ask them.
- **Stay off your phone:** Do we really have to say it? If you're looking at your phone during an interview, you'll look like you don't care. Nobody wants to hire someone who doesn't care before the job even starts!

WHAT TO WEAR

There's an old saying in business: "Don't dress for the job you have. Dress for the job you want." That's never more true than at a job interview!

So what should you wear for a job interview? The answer is easy—business clothes. A suit is always a good idea. If you don't have a suit, you should consider investing in at least one (if someone wants to buy you a graduation gift, this is an option!). If not, wear dress pants or skirt with a nice blazer-type jacket. Wear a solid-color shirt so your tie or scarf won't clash.

Professional dress is important in the business world. *Linda Raymond/E+/Getty Images*

You should be neatly groomed. Your hands should be clean, especially your fingernails. Your hair should be freshly washed and arranged in a neat and tidy way. Your clothes should be clean, pressed, and well fitting, without spots, rips, or tears. If you wear any jewelry, keep it to a minimum. If you have tattoos, keep them covered. Be sure your shoes are clean and polished. Avoid perfumes, colognes, or body sprays.

If you have a briefcase, put a few copies of your résumé in it, and bring it along.

WHAT EMPLOYERS LOOK FOR

Every business professional should have certain qualities. During a job interview, potential employers will be assessing you for these characteristics. Ask yourself these questions, and if you think you need to get better at something, then get better!

Bring your best self to work, and you'll be a welcome member of the team. *Xavierarnau/E+/Getty Images*

Communication and Social Skills

- Will you be able to understand customers' problems, needs, and values?
- Will you be able to work well with your boss and coworkers?
- Do you have active listening skills?
- Do you speak clearly?
- Do you write clearly?
- Do you show politeness, friendliness, and a good attitude?

Good Work Ethic

- Do you work hard at assigned tasks?
- Do you look for ways to help employers, coworkers, or customers beyond assigned tasks?
- Do you look for ways to improve your performance?
- Are you on time?
- Do you work well and thoroughly until the job is done (rather than watch the clock to see how soon you can leave)?
- Do you show initiative and work to solve problems?

Adaptability

- Are you flexible about new situations, new rules and regulations, new or different environments?
- Are you willing and eager to learn the latest developments, processes, procedures, and code updates?
- Can you get along with all kinds of people?

Enthusiasm for Your Field

- Do you feel good about the work you do?
- Do you like solving problems?
- Do you like helping people?
- Are you interested in advancement?
- Do you have a desire to continuing to build your skills and learn new things?

FOLLOWING UP

After any kind of job interview, it is *extremely important* to follow up. This is what shows the potential employer that you are genuinely interested in the job and in working with them. Write your thank-you note immediately after the interview. Not tomorrow, not later in the week, not sometime soon—*the same day*. E-mail is fine and the fastest way to say thank you. Be sure to mention your interest in the job and one or two things from the interview that interested you most. If you met separately with several people, *send each one of them a separate note*!

On the Job

Now that you've got the job, it's important to keep it! It's not that hard. Just remember these simple tips:

- **Do your best:** You biggest asset will always be high-quality work.
- **Be reliable:** Employers and colleagues want to know that they can count on you.
- **Be on time:** Show up for work on time or even a few minutes early.

- **Be prepared:** Walk in the door ready to work.
- **Keep good records:** This saves everyone time and money, from your boss to your customers to yourself.
- **Be polite:** Treat everyone you meet with the same respect you want to receive.
- **Stay calm:** You do your best work when you're calm, especially if you have a problem to solve. Sometimes other people can be difficult; if you stay calm, difficult situations are easier to resolve.
- **Have integrity:** Be honest and respect other people and their property.

Summary

The market is strong for all of the kinds of financial managers we've talked about in this book, and it will continue to be. Whether you work for a small business or a large corporation, a financial institution or insurance company, or a nonprofit organization, there will always be a need for someone to manage the finances and the financial team.

Good luck!

KEVIN WARD, INSURANCE MANAGER

Kevin Ward is an insurance manager for Turner Construction Company in Boston, Massachusetts. He studied at the University of Connecticut and holds a bachelor of business administration (BBA) degree from the University of North Texas with a focus on finance. His background includes working as a claims consultant and claims manager for insurance and construction companies.

Kevin Ward. *Courtesy of Kevin Ward*

What does an insurance manager for a company do?

We protect our business and our employees. I'm responsible for overseeing all of our construction projects in New England. I make sure our insurance is well-matched with the different risks of construction in our industry. I think of it like a jigsaw puzzle. Each insurance product could be considered a puzzle piece. By putting them together, you can protect the company against lawsuits or other problems. Whatever you can think of, there's an insurance product to protect against it.

How did you decide to become an insurance manager?

In college, I studied finance, and part of that core curriculum included some insurance and risk management classes. When I graduated in 2009, we were in the middle of the great recession, and no jobs were available. I'm from Hartford, Connecticut, the insurance capital of the world, so when I moved back there, I had more opportunities. My first job was in insurance claims at Hartford Insurance Company. I didn't really know anything, but I was fortunate to have a really good training program from the leadership in that group. Things like: What is coverage? What does the product give to the consumer? What do we agree to protect them from? How is fault determined? The litigation process, and how it varies in different jurisdictions.

For seven years, mastering the different pieces of insurance and litigation, I was particularly focused on general liability, which is the insurance that covers you when you cause bodily injury to someone else, for instance, asbestosis cases or exposure to lead paint. I worked with clients who bought insurance to protect them from these lawsuit scenarios. I also handled construction defect insurance—anything connected to construction projects. By growing that knowledge of how the pieces fit together, it opened up the opportunity to move from the insurer side to the insured side.

In 2016, I got an opportunity to move to Suffolk Construction, a large general contractor in the Boston market. It had really grown in the last few years and was looking to become a national general contractor, competing with the top twenty contractors in the country. They were looking to build a group to manage risk for the business. I was one of the first employees in that group. We built out procedures and protocols, like the time line for claim handling requisitions: How long do you have after something comes in to respond? Who has authority to settle? All the infrastructure of a claim-handling administration. We also handled all the claims that came in from across the country in many jurisdictions. It was a good opportunity to learn—you realize how little you know!

After three and a half years of doing that, I was promoted a couple of times. An opportunity arose to move to Turner Construction, the number one construction firm in the country, according to ENR (*Engineering News-Record*, the industry periodical that ranks contractors on many different measures). It was a good opportunity to take on additional responsibilities and grow my career beyond the claim-focused world into more of a holistic risk manager/insurance manager. So, in this role, in addition to the claim handling aspects, I also get to be responsible for making sure the insurance on every job across the northeast is correct. I review our insurance and the insurance we require of our subcontractors. Obviously, COVID is a hot topic right now; I'm very involved in our COVID response—determining what's an insurable response, what can we do to prepare, and what's recoverable.

What is a typical day on your job?

Every day is different. Some days it's contract review; some days it's meeting with our safety personnel. I handle our workers' compensation claims. Then we review lessons learned; we figure out what went wrong and what we can do better next time. Our safety professionals are project specific. I have a wider vantage point to see trends. I do some data analytics. I work with our financial and business managers to price insurance. We need to price our insurance competitively, so I work with our insurance brokers and risk management folks. That makes us more attractive as a builder, because our costs will be lower. We have a unique insurance program. The industry has gone to wrap-up programs where all the insurance is packaged by the company (CCIP or contractor-controlled insurance program). The risk that each of the contractors, subcontractors, and owners has on the job is usually covered by a hundred different plans. Turner provides one all-inclusive policy that's been built in a way that covers our major risks. So, we enroll all the parties on the job into our CCIP. Part of my job is selling the value of that product as a risk management tool. It reduces the administrative burden and makes the coverages uniform, so there's less infighting between parties, because we're all under the same umbrella.

What's the best part of being an insurance manager?

I like that I am central to everything, and every day is different. I interface with senior management, external customers; I partner with our project teams—the ones actually building the buildings. I can build those relationships and understand how the different pieces of the business fit together, because I'm kind of a central hub.

What's the most challenging part of being an insurance manager?

The part I like the least is the administrative tasks—keeping logs, the data entry stuff. It can be a high-conflict job, depending on the issues you're dealing with. Sometimes we might have to deny a worker a claim. Managing the human aspect of it, doing what's right but standing firm and putting your company's interests first—that can be challenging. Also, the breadth of the insurance industry is challenging. You could spend your whole career specializing in one line of coverage. In this role, because it touches so many pieces, you're not going to know all of it. You'll have to research it, and you're going to make mistakes. The role is bigger than you'll ever be.

What's the most surprising thing about an insurance manager?

Insurance is not a sexy industry. It's not something that draws people's attention. Most kids don't dream of being an insurance manager. The thing about insurance is there are so many opportunities, so many areas to specialize and learn, there are huge employment career paths that people just walk right past because they don't understand that they're there. A lot of the talent is aging out, so there are lots of opportunities for young people to learn, advance, and have a great career. It's an industry where you can do very well for yourself. You're not limited to just working for an insurance company. You can work for an insurer, or end up on the broker side, or on the consumer side, because we need to understand how the products work.

How did (or didn't) your education prepare you to be an insurance manager?

The general college education, learning to write and communicate is essential. Communication skills are everything. You need to be able to persuade people and have an impact. A lot of that comes from the reading and writing you do in your education. My degree gave me financial literacy, so I understand how a business makes money—their income and expenses. A lot of my job is shoring up the profitability of the business, and I can't do that if I don't understand the numbers. A lot of what I do is legal-adjacent, so understanding how the court system works, and the legal side is important. But if I had gotten my degree in English, I'd probably be nearly as prepared. Because college is about learning how to work, how to learn. So much of what you need to know about insurance specifically is what you learn on the job. What prepares you for your next role is learning things and waiting for them to coalesce.

Is being an insurance manager what you expected?

Largely, yes. When I took the role, I was familiar enough with it to know roughly what the responsibilities would be. You never really know what the day in the life is like until you live the day in the life, but it's a reasonable match to my expectations.

What's next? Where do you see yourself going from here?

I've only been in this role for eight months, so for the foreseeable future, I'm going to focus on learning the job and optimizing how well I can perform this role. That's the first step—master what you're doing now, and opportunities will arise as you demonstrate your confidence. Possible next steps—the person in my role before me was promoted to a national role overseeing several claim groups. Or another person moved to more of the insurance placement, where they work with the insurer to design the insurance product that we're buying and price it. Ultimately, another path would be a chief risk officer. That would encompass not only the insurance risk, but the other risks the company faces—it's a more holistic management position. You don't always have to continue up. Sometimes you find what works for you, and your career is a piece of your life, not your whole life. For me, having my family and my personal time—that balance is very important to me.

Where do you see the career of insurance manager going from here?

I think insurance as a whole is pretty stable. The industry is one of the slower movers, but technology is starting to take hold in the field. There will always be a need for insurance managers, particularly in construction where I'm focused, but in all industries. There's always going to be a need for a person to figure out how we can protect ourselves.

What is your advice for a young person considering this career?

Go for it! I think getting the education is important as a first step. A bachelor's degree is pretty much a prerequisite nowadays. A focus in finance or law or risk management would be optimal, but other degrees are fine. I've known people with degrees in English, history, mathematics. You can come from any degree and do well in this field. I think you have to have an innate quality to like to learn and figure things out, and to be open to opportunities. Do well at what you're doing, master it, keep your eyes open, and think about where you might go. I didn't have a specific plan; I just stayed open to opportunities. If you're a little uncomfortable, you'll work to do a good job. That's the key to really growing. And be kind. One thing that's overlooked is that the people who do the best are the ones who work well with others. I think at least 50 percent of my success is being kind, being willing to pitch in—I think that's a skill that's underrated.

MARTY MAYNARD, RISK MANAGER

Marty Maynard. *Courtesy of Marty Maynard*

Marty Maynard has served as risk manager for general government for the town of Windsor, Connecticut, since 2001. His office covers all municipal departments, for example, police, public works, recreation, fire, and so forth, as well as the board of education, making him responsible for services to more than 1,265 employees. He evaluates and manages the risk of loss associated with the town and board of education (different types of liability, worker compensation, and accident/health), provides safety training to employees, and serves as deputy fire marshal, providing backup services to the fire marshal and fire inspector. Maynard holds an associate's degree in fire science from Springfield Technical College and a BS in fire science and MS in industrial safety from the University of Central Missouri. He is a certified Connecticut municipal official (CCMO), is designated a management liability insurance specialist (IRMI), and holds numerous other certifications. His specialty areas are OSHA standards, firefighter safety, public sector safety, and municipal risk management.

What does a risk manager for a town do?

As risk manager for a municipality, I'm responsible for purchasing insurance needed by the town and board of education, all forms of property and casualty insurance, including general liability, property, casualty, and now cyber insurance and drone insurance (which covers any damage caused by a drone owned by the town or board of education). I also conduct field audits to ensure the safety of the town's personnel and make corrective recommendations. By far, my largest task is managing the workers' compensation program for the town and board of education, meaning I'm involved in all workers' compensation claims, and I'm responsible for managing the liability and property claims for the town and board of education.

How did you decide to become a risk manager?

There's a long story! For eleven years, I worked for the Connecticut liability municipal league pool and its insurance program. Four-fifths of the towns in the state belong to this insurance pool for workers' compensation, liability, auto, and so forth. I was a risk consultant, going out as the servicing representative to about one-fourth of the towns in the program. After doing that for a number of years, I thought maybe it was time for me to branch out; and instead of just giving the recommendations, I should work in a municipality and apply what I've learned throughout the years to my municipality. I was fortunate that Windsor was looking for a full-time risk manager. Not a lot of municipalities have full-time risk managers. In Connecticut, there are probably a dozen. But it's a field that's starting to open up, and more and more municipalities will be looking to have full-time risk managers. With all the issues we have today—COVID, workplace violence, cyber security issues, and cost containment —I think they'll be looking to hire more risk managers in the future.

What is a typical day on your job?

A typical day for me is to get in and check e-mails to see what happened the night before. Then working with my claims adjusters or my attorneys to manage claims. Reviewing medical management of workers' compensation claims, assisting the attorney general on property claims. I generally have time to do field audits. Then there's reviewing insurance contracts for proper insurance language. I respond to accidents involving town employees. So if a motor vehicle accident is reported, I'll go out to the scene, take notes and photographs, and work with the police to get all the information I need to take care of the employee and take care of the vehicle. Sometimes there's property damage from such things as a leaky toilet on the third floor of a building that leaks all the way down. I work with the insurance adjusters to mitigate the issue. That's one of the better parts of my job—that it's so varied.

What's the best part of being a risk manager?

The best part? You know, there are a couple of really great things. The job is varied. No two days are ever the same. I never sit at my desk all day just doing paperwork. There is paperwork, but I can also go out and see that things get repaired, things get fixed. The best part of my job is helping an injured employee get the treatment that he or she needs to get better. If an employee has to go to the hospital, I go to the hospital—twenty-four/seven. Sometimes they're all set, but sometimes I give them a ride home if no one has come to pick them up. I represent the employer, but I'm there for the employee. I love what I do.

What's the most challenging part of being a risk manager?

The other side of that is sometimes it's challenging going to the accident scene. Sometimes seeing the injured parties is pretty challenging. Talking with someone who has suffered a loss is very challenging. Sometimes there are challenges when it comes to a claim or a lawsuit, trying to explain to the person why there may not be any coverage for him or why the claim was denied, in some cases. That's probably the most challenging area.

What's the most surprising thing about being a risk manager?

Some of the thoughts and ideas that come up from different departments. For instance, I serve as deputy fire marshal. I had someone from another department who wanted to have a fire juggling demonstration. I had to let the person down gently and say we're trying to prevent fires and just don't think a municipality should have a fire juggling demonstration. Some ideas are great. For others, we have to consider the risk versus benefit to the organization. We try to tell them, "Great thought; let's keep thinking of different things, but let's move on." Now the hot-air balloon coming to a school—that was fine. I used to crew for a hot-air balloon. It's a little more of a controlled atmosphere.

How did (or didn't) your education prepare you to be a risk manager?

I started off studying fire science. I thought I was going to remain in the fire service. That portion of my education has always stayed with me and really does help in the job. The master's in industrial safety was critical in that I know a lot about the present OSHA regulations; I help the town comply with those regulations. Having an industrial safety degree means that I can do a lot of training myself, without having to hire outside vendors. There are some classes I should have taken in school, like accounting! Risk management involves a lot of numbers, between the budget and insurance. I've learned by dealing with it, but I didn't have a background in accounting or statistics while I was in college. That's an area I should have looked at.

Is being a risk manager what you expected?

In some cases, definitely yes. In some instances, I didn't expect to be called upon for certain issues. Overall, yes. It's a wonderful job. It's varied. You have a lot of input into a lot of different things, and you're helping the organization that you're working for.

What's next? Where do you see yourself going from here?

I've been here for almost twenty years, and I'll probably do another eight to ten years here. After that, I think I will retire. But that doesn't mean I'm hanging up my hat! I have a good background with municipal safety, and I'll probably do some consulting after I retire.

Where do you see the career of a risk manager going from here?

Risk management is only going to increase among corporations and municipalities. Both private and public sectors are finding risk management as a profession and as a tool. With liability issues and the need to mitigate risk, I only see the profession growing in numbers in the near future.

What is your advice for a young person considering this career?

A young person entering the field of risk management needs to have a good accounting background but also should have a background in insurance and safety. My advice is to seek out a risk manager and talk to him. Whether it's private sector or public sector, we all face the same challenges on a daily basis. It's an exciting field for a young person. Every day is different. Every day brings new challenges. I've been doing this a long time and, frankly, I'm amazed at what I see on a day-to-day basis.

Notes

Introduction

1. Idowu Koyenikan, *Wealth for All: Living a Life of Success at the Edge of Your Ability* (Fuquey-Varina, NC: Grandeur Touch, 2016), 25.

Chapter 1

1. Bureau of Labor Statistics (BLS), "Occupational Outlook Handbook—Financial Managers," updated September 1, 2020, https://www.bls.gov/ooh/management/financial-managers.htm#tab-2.

2. Idowu Koyenikan, *Wealth for All: Living a Life of Success at the Edge of Your Ability* (Fuquey-Varina, NC: Grandeur Touch, 2016), 5.

3. Indeed.com Career Guide, "Finance Manager Skills: Definition and Examples," October 19, 2020, https://www.indeed.com/career-advice/resumes-cover-letters/skills-required-for-finance-manager.

4. *U.S. News & World Report*, "Financial Manager Overview," October 27, 2020, from https://money.usnews.com/careers/best-jobs/financial-manager.

5. Bureau of Labor Statistics (BLS), "Occupational Outlook Handbook—Financial Managers—Job Outlook," updated September 1, 2020, https://www.bls.gov/ooh/management/financial-managers.htm#tab-6.

6. Bureau of Labor Statistics (BLS), "Occupational Outlook Handbook—Financial Managers—Pay," updated September 1, 2020, https://www.bls.gov/ooh/management/financial-managers.htm#tab-5.

7. Accounting.com Staff Writers, "What Is GAAP?" September 18, 2020, https://www.accounting.com/resources/gaap.

8. Will Kenton, "Branch Manager," *Investopedia Career Advice*, updated September 13, 2019, https://www.investopedia.com/terms/b/branch-manager.asp.

9. Salary.com, "Cash Manager," https://www.salary.com/research/job-description/benchmark/cash-manager-job-description#:~:text=Cash%20Manager%20responsibilities%20include%20managing,compliance%20to%20state%20financial%20laws.

10. Dave Robinson, "Controller vs. CFO: Which Does My Business Need?" *Driven Insights* [Blog], December 11, 2018, https://www.driveninsights.com /small-business-finance-blog/controller-vs-cfo-which-does-my-business-need.

11. OwlGuru, "How to Become a Compliance Manager," https://www.owlguru .com/career/compliance-managers/.

12. Robert Half, "Hot Jobs: What Does It Take to Be a Compliance Manager?" *Robert Half Blog*, September 29, 2015, https://www.roberthalf.com/blog/salaries -and-skills/hot-jobs-what-does-it-take-to-be-a-compliance-manager.

13. Robert Half, "What You Need to Know about Controller Salaries and Jobs," *Robert Half Blog*, July 1, 2020, https://www.roberthalf.com/blog/salaries-and-skills /all-you-need-to-know-about-controller-salary-levels-jobs#:~:text=A%20controller %20oversees%20an%20organization's,financial%20health%20of%20the%20firm.

14. Lisa McQuerrey, "The Role of a Credit Manager in a Bank," *Chron*, June 29, 2018, https://work.chron.com/role-credit-manager-bank-18271.html.

15. James Chen, "Fund Manager," *Investopedia*, updated March 25, 2020, https:// www.investopedia.com/terms/f/fundmanager.asp.

16. International Risk Management Institute (IRMI), "Risk Management: Definition," *IRMI Glossary*, https://www.irmi.com/term/insurance-definitions/risk -management.

17. Bureau of Labor Statistics, "Occupational Outlook Handbook—Financial Managers—Job Outlook."

Chapter 2

1. Clarity Recruitment, "7 Qualities of the Best People in Finance and Accounting," *Clarity Recruitment Blog, Career Advice*, May 25, 2020, https://finding clarity.ca/blog/7-qualities-of-the-best-people-in-finance-and-accounting/.

2. Clarity Recruitment, "7 Qualities of the Best People in Finance and Accounting"; Bureau of Labor Statistics (BLS), "How to Become a Financial Manager," *Occupational Outlook Handbook*, updated September 1, 2020, https:// www.bls.gov/ooh/management/financial-managers.htm#tab-4; Dan Butcher, "10 Personality Traits Needed to Succeed in Finance," *eFinancialCareers*, November 16, 2016, https://news.efinancialcareers.com/us-en/265717/the-top-10-soft-skills -and-personality-traits-that-hiring-managers-look-for.

3. Minnesota State CAREERWise, "Financial Managers: Education and Credentials," *Ready to Explore Careers?*, https://careerwise.minnstate.edu/careers /careerDetail?id=3&oc=113031.

4. Brian Witte, "Take 5 Steps to Find an Internship during High School," *U.S. News & World Report/Education/College Admissions Playbook*, February 16, 2015, https://www.usnews.com/education/blogs/college-admissions-playbook/2015/02/16/take-5-steps-to-find-an-internship-during-high-school.

Chapter 3

1. B. B. King, quoted outside the Main Library in uptown Charlotte, North Carolina, in the *Charlotte Observer*, October 5, 1997, 2D.

2. Kimiz Dalkir, *Knowledge Management in Theory and Practice*, 2nd ed. (Cambridge: Massachusetts Institute of Technology, 2011), 2.

3. Isaac Asimov, *The Roving Mind* (Amherst, NY: Prometheus, 1983), 116.

4. Benjamin Franklin and Benjamin Peirce, *Poor Richard's Almanac for [1850–52]: As Written by Benjamin Franklin, for the Years [1733–41]: The Astronomical Calculation*, annual illustrated ed. (New York: John Doggett Jr., 1849).

5. Jennifer Ma, Matea Pender, and C. J. Libass, *Trends in College Pricing 2020* (New York: College Board, 2020), https://research.collegeboard.org/pdf/trends-college-pricing-student-aid-2020.pdf.

6. BigFutureTM, "Focus on Net Price, Not Sticker Price," *College Board*, https://bigfuture.collegeboard.org/pay-for-college/paying-your-share/focus-on-net-price-not-sticker-price.

7. Edith Hamilton, quoted in the *Saturday Evening Post*, September 27, 1958.

8. Teddy Nykiel, "9 Money Tips for New College Grads," *NerdWallet*, May 10, 2019, https://www.nerdwallet.com/article/loans/student-loans/money-tips-college-graduates.

9. Nykiel, "9 Money Tips for New College Grads."

Glossary

annual report: a document that organizations prepare every year that must accurately describe their operations and financial condition.

baccalaureate degree: bachelor's degree.

bachelor's degree: a degree earned by a college or university student after completing a program that usually takes four years.

bank: a financial institution that is licensed to make loans and receive deposits and sometimes provide financial services and safe deposit boxes; includes retail banks, commercial/corporate banks, investment banks.

bankruptcy: a legal proceeding relating to a person or business that cannot pay their debts; provides debt relief to debtor while providing creditors with (some) repayment.

bond: an investment instrument that represents a loan from the investor to a borrower (government or company); used by companies and governments at all levels to finance projects and operations.

branch bank: a smaller, "storefront" location of a bank that is conveniently located away from the home office.

capital: funds held in special accounts, such as deposit or investment accounts; capital can be used to generate interest income or to fund a business expansion.

certificate: a document issued to show that a person has completed a process, earned or achieved a particular status.

certified management accountant (CMA): certification signifying expertise in financial accounting and strategic management.

certified public accountant (CPA): certification signifying expertise shown by education and experience requirements from the American Institute of

Certified Public Accountants (AICPA); other countries sometimes use the equivalent term "chartered accountant."

chartered financial analyst (CFA): international designation for financial analysts from the CFA Institute certifying competence and integrity.

chief executive officer (CEO): highest-ranking executive of an organization; responsible for making major decisions, managing overall operations/resources, and liaison to the board of directors.

chief financial officer (CFO): senior executive responsible for managing the financial actions of a company; role can be similar to treasurer or controller.

chief operating officer (COO): senior executive in charge of overseeing organization's day-to-day administrative and operational functions; typically, second in command to the CEO.

chronological: organized by date from oldest to newest (see reverse chronological).

compliance: the department ensures that the organization adheres to external rules and internal controls.

contact information: name, address, telephone number, e-mail address, or any other means to communicate with another person.

controller: senior executive who oversees the accounting operations of a company.

corporation: a legal entity that is separate and distinct from its owners but has most rights/responsibilities that individuals have.

cover letter: a business letter that goes with and explains a résumé or other enclosure.

credit: an agreement whereby a borrower promises to repay a lender at a later date, generally with interest; also, an individual or business's creditworthiness or credit history.

credit score: a number between 300 and 850 that lenders and financial institutions use to determine creditworthiness for an individual.

credit union: a financial cooperative that provides traditional banking services and is owned by its members, so it is a tax-exempt, not-for-profit entity.

C-suite (also called C-level): the group of most-important senior executives of a company; generally, CEO, CFO, COO, and CIO (chief information officer).

derivative: a financial security whose value relies on (is derived from) an asset or group of assets (benchmark); its price is based on fluctuations in that underlying asset.

diploma: official document awarded by an educational institution that indicates completion of a particular course of study; may or may not be associated with a degree.

embezzle: to steal or misappropriate funds belonging to one's employer placed in one's trust.

entrepreneur: a person who creates a new business, bears most of the risks, and reaps most of the rewards.

financial institution: an organization whose business is financial/monetary transactions (e.g., deposits, loans, investments, currency exchange); examples are banks, credit unions, trust companies, insurance companies, brokerage firms, and investment dealers.

financial instrument: assets that can be traded in the form of real or virtual documents that represent a legal agreement involving monetary value, including cash instruments and derivative instruments.

financial security: a tradable financial instrument that can be used to raise capital in financial markets; categories are equities (e.g., stocks), debts (e.g., bonds, certificates of deposit), and hybrid.

for-profit college: businesses that sell college-level coursework, sometimes leading to a diploma or degree, usually online; the goal is to generate a profit for owners or shareholders; sometimes engage in predatory student loan practices.

general education diploma (GED): a credential equivalent to a high-school diploma that is obtained through testing.

generally accepted accounting principles (GAAP): a set of rules covering the details, complexities, and legalities of business and corporate accounting.

hedge: an investment made in hopes of reducing risk of adverse price movement in an asset, as if taking out an insurance policy; hedging reduces potential risk but also reduces potential gains.

initial public offering (IPO): the first time that shares of a private company are offered for sale to the public as stock.

insurance: a contract (called a policy) where a person or organization receives financial protection or reimbursement against losses from an insurance company; used to hedge against financial risk and liability.

investment: an asset acquired in hopes of generating income or growth in value.

investment bank: a financial services company that acts as an intermediary in large and complex financial transactions, such as IPOs and mergers for corporate clients.

margin: money that is borrowed from a brokerage company to buy an investment; represents the difference between the investment's total value and the amount borrowed.

MBA: master of business administration degree.

municipality: a town or city with a local government.

mutual fund: investment portfolio made up of stocks, bonds, and other securities managed by an investment company with a fund manager making investment decisions on behalf of individual investors.

networking: forming and maintaining personal connections or relationships with people in your chosen field.

private college/university: a nonprofit college or university that does not receive funding from the state in which it is located; also called "independent" college/university.

public college/university: a nonprofit college (including community, technical, or four-year colleges) or university that receives some of its funding from the state in which it is located.

résumé: an organized list of professional qualifications and accomplishments.

revenue: income generated by normal business operations; gross income before expenses are subtracted.

reverse chronological: organized by date from newest to oldest (see chronological).

risk: possibility of injury or loss; in financial terms, risk is the chance that actual gains will be different from expected return; in insurance terms, the probability of financial loss from a specific cause or source.

SB: bachelor of science degree. SB is Latin for "scientiae baccalaureus"; SB is used by some institutions, and BS is used by others.

security: a negotiable financial instrument that has some kind of monetary value, such as stocks or bonds.

Securities and Exchange Commission (SEC): independent U.S. federal government regulatory agency responsible for protecting investors and regulating the securities markets.

start-up: a company in the early stages of operations.

stock: a security representing ownership of a fraction of a corporation entitling the owner to an equal fraction of the business's assets and profits; a "share" is a unit of stock.

Further Resources

*T*his section includes useful resources relating to financial management careers. This is not a complete list of all the information out there, but these resources will help you get started finding out more about the careers you're interested in.

College and Financial Aid

American Indian College Fund: Provides scholarships and college information for Native American students at any of the nation's thirty-three accredited tribal colleges and universities.
https://collegefund.org/

American Indian Graduate Center & AIGCS: Scholarship for Native American students in the United States at the high-school, undergraduate, and graduate levels.
https://www.aigcs.org/

APIA Scholars: Nonprofit organization that provides college scholarships for Asian Americans and Pacific Islanders (AAPI).
https://apiascholars.org/

Cappex: Free website where you can find out about colleges and merit aid scholarships.
https://www.cappex.com/

CashCourse: "Your real-life money guide." Provides financial information, education, and tools to help you learn about your financial options.
https://www.cashcourse.org

Chegg: Website with searchable information about scholarships and learn about colleges.
https://www.chegg.com/

Dell Scholars Program: Scholarship and college-completion program that helps students succeed.
https://www.dellscholars.org/

Fastweb: Searchable website for research on scholarships, internships colleges, and so forth.
https://www.fastweb.com

Gates Millennium Scholars: Provides scholarships to reduce barriers to college for African American, American Indian/Alaska Native, Asian Pacific Islander American, and Hispanic American students regardless of major.
https://gmsp.org/

GoCollege.com: Guide to free money with college scholarships.
www.gocollege.com/financial-aid/scholarships/types/

HS Finder (Hispanic Scholarship Fund): Helps Hispanic/Latinx students find scholarship information.
https://finder.hsf.net/

KnowHow2GO: Provides information for middle-school and high-school students, and veterans, on how to get ready for and go to college.
http://knowhow2go.acenet.edu/

National Society of High School Scholars (NSHSS): Connects students with scholarships, college fairs, internships, career and leadership opportunities, partner discounts, and more. All students are eligible to apply for high-school and college scholarships in the areas of academic excellence, entrepreneurship, leadership, literature, medicine, music, STEM, sustainability, visual arts, and more.
https://www.nshss.org

Peerlift: Provides information about scholarships, internships, summer programs, and more gathered by students.
http://www.peerlift.org

Scholar Snapp: Free data standard allowing students to reuse their application information for multiple scholarship applications.
https://www.scholarsnapp.org

Scholarship America: Website to research and apply for scholarships.
https://scholarshipamerica.org/

Scholarships.com: Free website to search for college scholarship and financial aid information.
https://www.scholarships.com/

Scholly: Mobile app to find scholarships for college.
https://myscholly.com

Thurgood Marshall College Fund: Provides scholarships for students at any of the forty-seven public historically black colleges and universities (HBCUs), as well as support for the institutions. Occasionally, it offers scholarships to other schools.
https://www.tmcf.org/

UNCF: Awards scholarships and internships to students from low- and moderate-income families for college tuition, books, and room and board. The website also has tips for applying for other scholarships.
https://uncf.org/

Credentialing Organizations

Certified management accountant (CMA)
Awarded by the Institute of Management Accountants
www.imanet.org

Certified public accountant (CPA)
Awarded by the American Institute of Certified Public Accountants (AICPA)
www.aicpa.com

Chartered financial analyst (CFA)
Awarded by the CFA Institute
www.cfainstitute.org

Financial Industry Regulatory Authority (FINRA)
Offers licensing examinations for a variety of subjects in the financial and securities industries
www.finra.org

Professional Associations and Organizations

The many, many organizations for financial managers vary by specialty, type of industry, and level of advancement. This list represents some of the top organizations you should know about but is not a comprehensive list of every professional association or organization relating to this field.

American Association of Bank Directors (AABD)

http://aabd.org/

AABD serves the information, education, and advocacy needs of individual bank and savings institution directors.

American Bankers Association (ABA)

https://www.aba.com/

ABA acts as the voice for big and small banks throughout the United States, providing advocacy, education and training, and expertise.

American Finance Association (AFA)

https://afajof.org

AFA is a global resource and advocate for the finance profession and is devoted to the study and promotion of knowledge about financial economics. It provides a professional community for the exchange of ideas with academics and professionals in the field of finance.

Association for Financial Professionals (AFP)

https://www.afponline.org/

AFP is a group of professional organizations for treasury and finance professionals. It offers professional certifications, conferences, training and education, industry news and publications, and an interactive community.

Association of Government Accountants (AGA)

https://www.agacgfm.org/

AGA is a member organization for government financial management professionals. It provides training events, continuing education, professional certification, industry news, and a code of ethics.

Bankers Association for Finance and Trade (BAFT)
BAFT is an international transaction banking association. It provides advocacy, thought leadership, education and training, and a global forum for its members in the areas of trade finance, payments, compliance, and regulations.

Consumer Bankers Association (CBA)
https://www.consumerbankers.com/
CBA is the trade association for retail banking. It provides advocacy, education, and promotion for the retail banking industry.

Financial Management Association (FMA)
https://www.fma.org/
FMA is an international professional association with the mission of broadening common interests between academics and practitioners in financial management. It provides opportunities for professional interaction, promotes basic and applied research on sound financial practices, and enhances finance education. Members have access to conferences, a member directory, job placement services, journals and other publications, and an extensive library of information on a wide variety of financial management topics.

Healthcare Financial Management Association (HFMA)
https://www.hfma.org/
HFMA is a membership organization for health-care financial management executives and leaders. It provides education, industry analyses, career development, events, and various tools and resources.

Institute of Financial Operations (IFO)
https://myfinancialops.org/
IFO is a membership-based association serving the financial operations ecosystem, with a focus on the accounts payable discipline.

National Association of Credit Managers (NACM)
https://nacm.org/

NACM is a professional organization for credit and financial executives for manufacturers, wholesalers, financial institutions, and varied service organizations. It provides a variety of services, resources, and education, as well as industry information and trade journals.

National Society of Compliance Professionals (NSCP)
https://nscp.org/
NSCP is a membership organization serving compliance professionals in the financial services industry, providing access to resources, including a community of like-minded peers, continuing education, and regulatory involvement through representation of compliance interests.

Professional Risk Managers' International Association (PRMIA)
https://www.prmia.org/
PRMIA is a nonprofit professional association for risk industry professionals. It provides certification at different levels, continuing education, networking opportunities, and industry news and information.

Society of Financial Service Professionals (FSP)
https://national.societyoffsp.org/
FSP is a multidisciplinary community of accomplished credentialed financial service professionals who provide such services as financial planning, estate planning, and more.

Other Useful Books and Websites

INFORMATION ABOUT ALL KINDS OF CAREERS

Bureau of Labor Statistics Occupational Outlook Handbook
https://www.bls.gov/ooh/

EXPERT ADVICE ON HOW TO BE SUCCESSFUL

The Really, Really Successful Manager: Building a Highly Motivated Team for Peak Performance
by Nancy Banks-Lear and John Banks-Lear
Available as a Kindle e-book from Amazon.com

The Bankers' Handbook
by William H. Baughn and Thomas L. Storrs
Irwin Professional Publishers; subsequent edition April 1, 1988
The ultimate handbook for anyone seriously interested in banking or becoming
   a banker.

Financial Management: Theory and Practice (16th ed.)
by Eugene F. Brigham and Michael C. Ehrhardt
Provides key theoretical concepts, along with practical tools, to make effective
   financial decisions and emphasizes corporate valuation and its relevance to
   financial decisions.

Soundview Magazine's **25 Best Leadership Books of All Time (as of July
   18, 2019)**
www.summary.com/magazine/the-25-best-leadership-books-of-all-time

MORE INFORMATION ABOUT INTERNSHIPS

Intern Match
internmatch.io

Internship Programs
www.internshipprograms.com

SEARCH FOR JOBS AND POST YOUR RÉSUMÉ

Careerbuilder.com
Indeed.com
Linkedin.com
Monster.com

Bibliography

Accounting.com Staff Writers. "What Is GAAP?" September 18, 2020. https://www.accounting.com/resources/gaap.

American Finance Association (AFA). "About the AFA." https://afajof.org/about-the-afa/.

Asimov, Isaac. *The Roving Mind*. Amherst, NY: Prometheus, 1983.

Association for Financial Professionals (AFP). "About." https://www.afponline.org/.

Association of Government Accountants (AGA). "About AGA." https://www.agacgfm.org/.

Bureau of Labor Statistics (BLS). "Financial Managers." *Occupational Outlook Handbook*. Updated September 1, 2020. https://www.bls.gov/ooh/management/financial-managers.htm.

———. "Financial Managers—Job Outlook." *Occupational Outlook Handbook*. Updated September 1, 2020. https://www.bls.gov/ooh/management/financial-managers.htm#tab-6.

———. "Financial Managers—Pay." *Occupational Outlook Handbook*. Updated September 1, 2020. https://www.bls.gov/ooh/management/financial-managers.htm#tab-5.

———. "How to Become a Financial Manager." *Occupational Outlook Handbook*. Updated September 1, 2020. https://www.bls.gov/ooh/management/financial-managers.htm#tab-4.

———. "Occupational Outlook Handbook—Financial Analysts." Updated September 1, 2020. https://www.bls.gov/ooh/business-and-financial/financial-analysts.htm#tab-2.

Butcher, Dan. "10 Personality Traits Needed to Succeed in Finance." *eFinancialCareers*. November 16, 2016. https://news.efinancialcareers.com/us-en/265717/the-top-10-soft-skills-and-personality-traits-that-hiring-managers-look-for.

Chen, James. "Fund Manager." *Investopedia*. Updated March 25, 2020. https://www.investopedia.com/terms/f/fundmanager.asp.

Clarity Recruitment. "7 Qualities of the Best People in Finance and Accounting." *Clarity Recruitment Blog, Career Advice*. May 25, 2020. https://finding clarity.ca/blog/7-qualities-of-the-best-people-in-finance-and-accounting/.

Financial Management Association (FMA). "Mission and History." https://www.fma.org/mission-and-history.

Franklin, Benjamin, and Benjamin Peirce. *Poor Richard's Almanac for [1850– 52]: As Written by Benjamin Franklin, for the Years [1733–41]: The Astronomical Calculations.* Annual illustrated ed. New York: John Doggett Jr., 1849.

Goodwin, Kimberly. "How the Location Quotient Works." *Property Metrics*. February 21, 2018. https://propertymetrics.com/blog/location-quotient/.

Grant, Mitchell. "Chief Financial Officer (CFO)." *Investopedia Business Leaders*. Updated July 28, 2020. https://www.investopedia.com/terms/c/cfo.asp #:~:text=A%20chief%20financial%20officer%20(CFO,weaknesses%20 and%20proposing%20corrective%20actions.

Half, Robert. "Hot Jobs: What Does It Take to Be a Compliance Manager?" *Robert Half Blog.* September 29, 2015. https://www .roberthalf.com/blog/salaries-and-skills/hot-jobs-what-does-it-take-to -be-a-compliance-manager.

———. "What You Need to Know About Controller Salaries and Jobs." *Robert Half Blog*. July 1, 2020. https://www.roberthalf.com/blog/salaries-and-skills /all-you-need-to-know-about-controller-salary-levels-jobs#:~:text=A%20 controller%20oversees%20an%20organization's,financial%20health%20 of%20the%20firm.

Healthcare Financial Management Association (HFMA). "About Us." https://www.hfma.org/about-hfma.html.

International Risk Management Institute (IRMI). "Risk Management: Definition." *IRMI Glossary.* https://www.irmi.com/term/insurance-defini tions/risk-management.

Investopedia. *Dictionary.* https://www.investopedia.com/financial-term-dic tionary-4769738.

JobHero. "Bank Manager Job Description." https://www.jobhero.com/job -description/examples/banking/manager.

Kenton, Will. "Branch Manager." *Investopedia Career Advice.* Updated September 13, 2019. https://www.investopedia.com/terms/b/branch-man ager.asp.

King, B. B., quoted outside the Main Library in uptown Charlotte, North Carolina, *Charlotte Observer*, October 5, 1997, 2D.

Koyenikan, Idowu. *Wealth for All: Living a Life of Success at the Edge of Your Ability.* Fuquay-Varina, NC: Grandeur Touch, 2016.

Ma, Jennifer, Matea Pender, and C. J. Libassi. *Trends in College Pricing 2020.* New York: College Board, 2020. https://research.collegeboard.org/pdf /trends-college-pricing-student-aid-2020.pdf.

Marohn, Charles. "The Real Reason Your City Has No Money." *Strong Towns.* January 10, 2017. https://www.strongtowns.org/journal/2017/1/9/the-real -reason-your-city-has-no-money.

McQuerrey, Lisa. "The Role of a Credit Manager in a Bank." *Chron.* June 29, 2018. https://work.chron.com/role-credit-manager-bank-18271.html.

Miller, Kelsey. "What Does an Accountant Do? Role, Responsibilities, and Trends." *Northeastern University* [Blog]. September 6, 2019. https://www. northeastern.edu/bachelors-completion/news/what-does-an-account ant-do/#:~:text=An%20accountant%20is%20a%20professional ,businesses%20and%20organizations%20employing%20them.

National Association of Credit Management (NASM). "About NASM." https://nacm.org/.

National Society of Compliance Professionals (NSCP). "About NSCP." https:// nscp.org/.

Nich, C. *Financial Management Majors Guide.* WorldWideLearn. 2020. https://www.worldwidelearn.com/online-education-guide/business/finan cial-management-major.htm.

OwlGuru. "How to Become a Compliance Manager." https://www.owlguru .com/career/compliance-managers/.

Professional Risk Managers' International Association (PRMIA). "About." https://www.prmia.org/.

Robinson, Dave. "Controller vs. CFO: Which Does My Business Need?" *Driven Insights* [Blog]. December 11, 2018. https://www .driveninsights.com/small-business-finance-blog/controller-vs-cfo -which-does-my-business-need.

Rouse, Margaret. "Definition: Financial Controller." *TechTarget.* Updated July 2013. https://searcherp.techtarget.com/definition/financial-controller.

Salary.com. "Cash Manager." https://www.salary.com/research/job-description /benchmark/cash-manager-job-description.

————. "Insurance Risk Manager." https://www.salary.com/research/job-description/benchmark/insurance-risk-manager-job-description.

Severson, Dana. "What Are Some Disadvantages of Being a Financial Manager?" *Career Trend.* Updated January 1, 2019. https://careertrend.com/good-bad-things-being-financial-advisor-37804.html.

Staples, Kathy. "Considerations for Choosing an MS vs. an MBA Program." *Peterson's.* June 10, 2020. https://www.petersons.com/blog/considerations-for-choosing-an-ms-vs-an-mba-program/.

Tuovila, Alicia. "Generally Accepted Accounting Principles (GAAP)." *Investopedia.* Updated April 20, 2020. https://www.investopedia.com/terms/g/gaap.asp.

U.S. News & World Report. "Financial Manager Overview." https://money.usnews.com/careers/best-jobs/financial-manager.

White, Sarah K. "What Is an IT Auditor? A Vital Role for Risk Assessment." *CIO Magazine*, March 5, 2019.

Witte, Brian. "Take 5 Steps to Find an Internship during High School." *U.S. News & World Report/Education/College Admissions Playbook.* February 16, 2015. https://www.usnews.com/education/blogs/college-admissions-playbook/2015/02/16/take-5-steps-to-find-an-internship-during-high-school.

ZipRecruiter. "What Is the Role of an Insurance Manager?" https://www.ziprecruiter.com/e/What-Is-the-Role-of-an-Insurance-Manager.

About the Author

Marcia Santore is an author and artist from New England. She enjoys writing about interesting people and the fascinating things they do. She has written on many topics, including profiles of artists, scholars, scientists, and businesspeople. She has also illustrated and published several children's books. See her writing website at www.amalgamatedstory.com and her artwork at www.marciasantore.com.

Made in United States
North Haven, CT
10 February 2022

15951048R00083